PENGUIN BOOKS

Selected Poems

Dylan Marlais Thomas was born in 1914 in Swansea. His father was senior English master at the Grammar School, where Dylan Thomas received his only formal education before becoming for eighteen months a reporter on the local newspaper. His early poetry matured quickly in private notebooks, and 1934 saw the publication of the twenty-year-old's first volume, *18 Poems*. Thereafter, bohemian literary life in London alternated with more positively creative periods back in Wales, but his London reputation also laid the base for a celebrated career in the 1940s and early 1950s as a writer for radio and film. Meanwhile, his second and third volumes – *Twenty-five Poems* (1936) and *The Map of Love* (1939) – consolidated his standing as a poet. In 1937 he married Caitlin Macnamara and in 1938 settled for the first time in Laugharne, the Carmarthenshire seaside village now most closely associated with his name, and a profound influence on his final works. Even at the end of the 1930s, holiday memories of rural Carmarthenshire joined native urban memories of Swansea in the autobiographical short stories of *Portrait of the Artist as a Young Dog* (1940). The relatively few poems written during the war years are still among the finest anti-war poems of the century; and 1944–5, spent partly at New Quay on the Cardiganshire coast, was an *annus mirabilis* of remembrances of childhood in poetry and prose. *Deaths and Entrances* in 1946 confirmed his status as a major lyric poet.

Between 1946 and 1949, with proximity to London for film and broadcasting work, the family lived in or near Oxford. 1949 saw a return to Laugharne, to the now famous Boat House. From 1950 on, the poet's attention was given mainly to completing *Under Milk Wood*, a 'Play for Voices' that had grown out of his work for radio and film, and from his experience of New Quay and Laugharne. His growing renown led to four lecturing tours of the United States, where a collection of late poems, *In Country Sleep*, was published in 1952. The same year saw the publication of his *Collected Poems 1934–1952*, to wide acclaim. *Under Milk Wood* received its first readings with actors at the Poetry Center of the Young Men's and Young Women's Hebrew Association in New York in May and October 1953. Dylan Thomas died in New York on 9 November 1953 from excessive drinking and medical mistreatment. He is buried at Laugharne.

Walford Davies was educated at the University of Oxford and was formerly Senior Lecturer in English Literature at St Anne's College, Oxford. He holds a personal chair in English Literature of the University of Wales and is currently Visiting Professor of English in the University of Rio Grande, Ohio.

He is the author of two critical studies of Dylan Thomas (*Dylan Thomas*, Open University Press, 1986 and *Dylan Thomas*, University of Wales Press, 1990). Amongst other volumes, he has edited (for Dent, unless otherwise stated): *Dylan Thomas: Early Prose Writings* (1971), *New Critical Essays* (1972), *Wordsworth: Selected Poems* (1974), *Gerard Manley Hopkins: The Major Poems* (1979), *Thomas Hardy: Selected Poems* (1982), *Dylan Thomas: The Collected Stories* (1983), *Deaths and Entrances* (Gregynog Press, 1984), *Dylan Thomas: Selected Poems* (1993), *Gerard Manley Hopkins: Poetry and Prose* (1999), and, with Ralph Maud, *Dylan Thomas: Collected Poems 1934–1953* (1988) and *Under Milk Wood* (1995).

The present new edition of Dylan Thomas's *Selected Poems* is a companion volume to Walford Davies's new Penguin edition of *Under Milk Wood*.

DYLAN THOMAS

Selected Poems

Edited with an Introduction and Notes by Walford Davies

PENGUIN BOOKS

PENGUIN BOOKS

Published by the Penguin Group
Penguin Books Ltd, 80 Strand, London WC2R 0RL, England
Penguin Putnam Inc., 375 Hudson Street, New York, New York 10014, USA
Penguin Books Australia Ltd, 250 Camberwell Road, Camberwell, Victoria 3124, Australia
Penguin Books Canada Ltd, 10 Alcorn Avenue, Toronto, Ontario, Canada M4V 3B2
Penguin Books India (P) Ltd, 11 Community Centre, Panchsheel Park, New Delhi – 110 017, India
Penguin Books (NZ) Ltd, Cnr Rosedale and Airborne Roads, Albany, Auckland, New Zealand
Penguin Books (South Africa) (Pty) Ltd, 24 Sturdee Avenue, Rosebank 2196, South Africa

Penguin Books Ltd, Registered Offices: 80 Strand, London WC2R 0RL, England

www.penguin.com

This selection published in Penguin Classics 2000

5

Copyright © The Trustees for the Copyrights of Dylan Thomas,
1933, 1934, 1936, 1939, 1946, 1952, 1954, 2000
Introduction and editorial material © Walford Davies, 2000
All rights reserved

The moral right of the author has been asserted

Set in 10/12.5 pt Monotype Garamond
Typeset by Rowland Phototypesetting Ltd, Bury St Edmunds, Suffolk
Printed in England by Clays Ltd, St Ives plc

Contents

Acknowledgements

Grateful thanks are extended to the Trustees for the copyright of the late Dylan Thomas for permission to publish the poems in this selection, and to the following institutions for help with textual sources and information: the Department of Manuscripts of the British Library; the Library of the University of Chicago; the Harry Ransom Humanities Research Center of the University of Texas; the Houghton Library of Harvard University; the Lilly Library of Indiana University; the Special Collection Library of the State University of New York at Buffalo; the Library of Ohio State University; the Pierpont Morgan Library.

More specifically, the editor wishes to acknowledge the pleasure and benefit of collaboration with Professor Ralph Maud on *Collected Poems 1934–1953*, Dent, 1988, the now standard edition on which the text of the great majority of these poems is based. Pleasure and benefit have also come over the years from the opportunity to discuss Dylan Thomas's poetry with many friends and colleagues, the following in particular: Dr John Ackerman; Professor Beatrice Batson, Wheaton College, Illinois; Dorothy Bednarowska, St Anne's College, Oxford; Gilbert Bennett of the Dylan Thomas Society of Great Britain; Professor John Carey, Merton College, Oxford; Paul Ferris, the poet's biographer; Professor Barbara Hardy, London University; Professor Emrys Jones, New College, Oxford; the late Professor Gwyn Jones, the University of Wales; Professor Charlotte Otten, Calvin College, Michigan; Professor Christopher Ricks, Boston University; the late Professor John Wain; Jeff Towns; Jason Walford Davies; Damian Walford Davies.

The editor also gratefully acknowledges the British Academy for funding in aid of research.

Introduction

Craftsmen don't put their products in the attic.

(Dylan Thomas, 'Poets on Poetry')

The writing of Introductions or Prefaces to his work was something Dylan Thomas himself found difficult. 'I can't write an ordinary prose-preface at all,' he wrote to his agent David Higham in June 1952, 'having no interest whatsoever in it.' He felt that his poems had already found their achieved form and that anything that diluted their concreteness by way of preamble, paraphrase or promotion in prose was unnecessary and potentially misleading. Of course, this resistance applied only when he himself was asked to write the preamble, the paraphrase or the promotion. Living as he did most of his life in penury, and being only human, he was in fact thankful for any promotion, as long as it helped him live to write another poem.

But there was also a deeper critical edge to this resistance to the abstract. It is, for example, no accident that the majority of the poems use only their own first lines as titles. Thomas felt that more generalized titles are a disservice: they simply give away synopses ahead of the poems' own narratives. First-line titles make you start again – at the very beginning. The same went for paraphrases. When Edith Sitwell gave an appreciative, but purely atmospheric, account of one of Thomas's 'Altarwise' sonnets, he lamented that she was not reading the sonnet 'literally' enough. He was too kind a man to refuse a more lowly reader's request to explain, but even then, when lured to furnish his own paraphrase, he always managed craftily to render the poem again in its own terms. In all this he was only applying to the reader his one test for a poet – that he or she should write 'out of', not 'towards' words. 'Have

I ever told you,' he asked Pamela Hansford Johnson in May 1934, 'of the theory of how all writers either work towards or away from words? Even if I have, I'll tell it to you again because it's true. Any poet or novelist you like to think of – he either works *out of* words or in the direction of them.' The formula, returned to again and again in Thomas's letters and critical writings, ironically places him in league with F. R. Leavis, the one major critic who stood out against the Welsh Dylan's achievement, as he oddly stood out against even the English Milton in the same terms – for exhibiting 'a feeling *for* words rather than a capacity for feeling *through* words; we are often, in reading him, moved to comment that he is "external" or that he "works from the outside"'. But Thomas's interest in all this was that of a practitioner, not of a critic. Though he was himself an astute critic in reviews of books and in broadcasts about other writers, his lectures in America at the end of his life were not 'lectures' at all but quickly-taken routes into the reading of actual poems, whether his own or those of other memorable poets. His favourite opening flourish at each venue was 'I am going to read aloud . . .'

The prefatory note that he did manage to write for the *Collected Poems* in 1952 shows the rightness of resisting even prefatory notes. It trapped him into saying:

> I read somewhere of a shepherd who, when asked why he made, from within fairy rings, ritual observances to the moon to protect his flocks, replied: 'I'd be a damn' fool if I didn't!' These poems, with all their crudities, doubts, and confusions, are written for the love of Man and in praise of God, and I'd be a damn' fool if they weren't.

This piece of space-saving archness was itself a waste of space, and Thomas knew it. As William Empson – this time a major critic *and* one of Thomas's greatest admirers – said in a related context: 'he knew all that kind of thing very well and could be distressed only by a refusal to say it.' Talk of fairy rings just doesn't *sound* like the man who wrote 'The force that through the green fuse drives the flower' or 'The hunchback in the park' or 'Over Sir John's hill'. But the unattended comment to John Malcolm Brinnin, that his poems were 'poems in praise of God's world by a man who doesn't believe in God', does.

Left to himself on less public occasions, he came up with wonderfully sharp insights, each one an excellent preface-in-miniature. For example, his naughty upsetting of the balance in claiming that 'I am not interested in poetry, only in poems'. Or his own genuine *sense* of balance in wanting his poetry to be, in a wonderful phrase, 'heavy in tare, though nimble'. That 'tare' is not the troublesome plant of the Bible but the solid form and carriage of the poetry. He had obviously plenty of important things to write about in introduction to his poetry. And yet in seeking to provide, at his publishers' request, a prose preface to the *Collected Prose* in 1952, he struggled and failed. But 'failed' is not the right word. He came up instead with an alternative – a poem, titled 'Prologue'. This now also stands at the head of this present selection. Anyone else would have found the 'Prologue' a thing infinitely more difficult to write than a prose preface. It has 102 lines. The first line rhymes with the last, and so on inwards until the exact middle of the poem is a rhyming couplet. And it was difficult for Thomas, too: 'Why I acrosticked myself like this,' he said, 'don't ask me.' But, however difficult to produce, it was at least a new poem, not a rationalization of poems already written. And, more important, its heavy 'tare' is also 'nimble'. The image established in the first two lines is of the day and the summer 'winding down' at summer's end. So when the first fifty-one lines have themselves 'wound down' to couple in a couplet (and rise again) with the second fifty-one, it is no accident that they do so in the line 'To Wales in my arms'. Beyond craft, but made possible only by craft, the line has a wonderful sense of cradling, embracing, fielding.

And 'Prologue' is anything but an extreme example. It introduces a body of poems most of which are just as strenuously crafted. This concern with intricate form was the result of a poetic temperament shaped at least partly by the poet's Welsh cultural background. Even though the first language of both his parents was Welsh, Thomas's father decided to deny that language to his son. But the Welsh language still surrounded the poet, along with people (his own father amongst them) able to tell him of the difficult verse-forms of classic Welsh strict-metre poetry. He once told Glyn Jones that, had he been able to write in Welsh, that is exactly the kind of poetry he would have written in that language, too. And there are numerous examples that show him consciously approximating in English to the rules of the Welsh-language tradition, even without knowing the full rules. For him it was not a matter of rule but of role. The equivalent exclamation to Thomas's 'Why I acrosticked myself like this, don't ask me' is therefore Gerard Manley Hopkins's equally bitter-sweet reflection 'I have made verse so laborious', because Hopkins, too, was a poet structuring an English poetry within earshot of the Welsh. So if we think that, because it goes unnoticed, the difficult rhyme-scheme of 'Prologue' cannot be doing any work, we should remember that, in certain traditions, the form of the poem is not there for us reading but for the poet writing. Recently, Seamus Heaney has spoken of the phenomenon as 'breaking stones for pleasure'. We are in the presence, not of a commentator leaning over to select some ready-made form vaguely appropriate to what he wants to say, but of a *maker*.

The emphasis in any preface to Dylan Thomas's poems falls therefore on the poet's craft and hard work. Of course, as Thomas himself put it,

> the magic in a poem is always accidental. No poet would labour intensively upon the intricate craft of poetry unless he hoped that, suddenly, the accident of magic would occur ... And the best poem is that whose worked-upon unmagical passages come closest, in texture and intensity, to those moments of magical accident.

But it remains a wonderful paradox that Thomas, hailed as one of the greatly 'inspired' lyrical poets of the twentieth century, and a so-called bohemian to boot, is at base a careworn technician. W. B. Yeats would have told us not to be surprised: 'The poet who writes the poem,' Yeats said, 'is never the bundle of accident and incoherence that sits down to breakfast.' Thomas was modest enough not to think that that claim should come from him personally in a prose preface. More privately, however, he was right to emphasize it. When Stephen Spender, in a review of *Twenty-five Poems* in the Communist *Daily Worker* in 1936, said that Thomas's poetry 'is turned on like a tap', the twenty-three-year-old coolly put the record straight:

> Spender's remark is really the exact opposite of what is true. My poems *are* formed; they are not turned on like a tap at all, they are

'watertight compartments'. Much of the obscurity is due to rigorous compression; the last thing they do is to flow; they are much rather hewn. Now Spender himself has no idea of form; his poetry is so much like poetry, and so remote from poems, that I think most of his work will become almost as unreadable as the worst of the Georgians – and very soon.

(to Henry Treece, 16 May 1938)

The fact that behind the apparent flow of Thomas's poems lie structures formed as if hewn out of stone is something the poems themselves clearly show. It is also what many of them keep on telling us. Long before he wrote 'Prologue', many of the poems were themselves already miniature 'prefaces' to the poetry, carrying his thoughts on writing. 'In my craft or sullen art' (1945), for example:

> In my craft or sullen art
> Exercised in the still night
> When only the moon rages . . .

Thomas slides the adjective 'sullen' along the line from *craft* on to *art*. Poetry, he implies, is essentially a craft; if it is an art at all, it is a 'sullen' art – a dark, morose one. Suddenly, Keats's idea that if poetry doesn't come 'as naturally as leaves to a tree, it had better not come at all' is questioned. But Keats did say 'as naturally', not 'as easily'. For Keats, as for Shakespeare or Hopkins or Thomas, individual words, images, rhythms and poetic forms also have their own 'natures'. Why should we imagine that any natural thing comes easily? That thought comes well from Dylan Thomas who, amongst many impressive landscape poems, also celebrates a more obscure 'nature'. His major themes are the resistant void out of which the world was first created, the strenuous forces by which it continues to grow, and the slow, coiled struggles of prenatal life that produce the men and women able to experience the world in the first place. The aim is to match external creativity with external craft. It is not surprising therefore that at the end of the very last line of 'In my craft or sullen art' Thomas slides the word 'art' out even further, out on a limb – out into limbo, even:

> Nor heed my craft or art.

His own beautifully morose reading of the poem on record effects a dramatic pause (indeed, a second caesura) after 'craft'. It is one of the great conceptual breaks between 'craft' and 'art' in poetry.

Seeing (or hearing) the word 'art' drop, like that, off the last edge of the poem highlights instead the poem's craft. But again the tare is nimble. The poem has a regular count of seven syllables per line, except where the final line of each of the two stanzas reduces itself to six syllables in a musical closure, and where one line –

> On these spindrift pages

– reduces itself to six syllables to mime its own reduced meaning: 'these *spindrift* pages'. In the same way the poem scatters divorced words that are clearly meant to reassemble in the reader's mind as brilliantly disturbed clichés. 'Ivory stages' and 'towering dead', for example: though they are seven lines apart, they yield 'ivory towers', a phrase not actually said by the poem – but heard, half heard, as the rarefied opposite of the workaday plod that went to the poem's making. And the whole is beautifully modulated to end off with the very words 'craft' and 'art' with which it started. That is exactly what makes them key words. Circularity of this kind is a major strength in poetry as it is not in, say, philosophy or science or journalism. The snake has its tail in its mouth.

And yet, though always delighting in craft, Thomas was ready to temper and query it. He was even ready to mistrust it. The 1938 poem 'Once it was the colour of saying' is again in effect about itself – though to say that such wonderfully powerful poems are 'about themselves' is to do an injustice to their power as poems in their own right. This is as true of 'Once it was the colour of saying' as it is of Empson's 'Let it Go', Hopkins's sonnet 'To R.B.', Coleridge's 'Dejection: An Ode' and, for that matter, even Wordsworth's *Prelude*. What they all have in common is the new conscious power that comes from finding that an old unselfconscious power has come to an end.

> Once it was the colour of saying
> Soaked my table the uglier side of a hill
> With a capsized field where a school sat still
> And a black and white patch of girls grew playing;

The gentle seaslides of saying I must undo
That all the charmingly drowned arise to cockcrow and kill.
When I whistled with mitching boys through a reservoir park
Where at night we stoned the cold and cuckoo
Lovers in the dirt of their leafy beds,
The shade of their trees was a word of many shades
And a lamp of lightning for the poor in the dark;
Now my saying shall be my undoing,
And every stone I wind off like a reel.

Thomas takes to task the dangerous autonomy of his craft. And true to form – or rather *un*true to form – the poem deconstructs itself before our very eyes, ending off as a fractured sonnet. It is one line short of fourteen. Its tidily achieved opening quatrain becomes only the ghost of a quatrain in its next four lines, and its two final rhyming words are allowed to run into sand, as it were, too far away from what they echo. But when Vernon Watkins raised what he called this 'error of shape', Thomas replied that 'the form was consistently emotional and I can't change it without a change of heart'. So the heart is involved in craft even when both are broken. This is the commitment – what Gerard Manley Hopkins called the 'being in earnest' – that makes the poems created, not merely assembled, things.

Behind the concern with craft, then, a concern *about* craft. In 'Once it was the colour of saying' Thomas at twenty-four (the age at which T. S. Eliot, another major admirer, thought *every* poet should change) is querying the most radical thing that a poet can query: form itself. Are the intricacy and the music making better, or merely getting-the-better-of, what he or she wants to say? Looking back in 'The Circus Animals' Desertion', Yeats realized that 'Players and painted scene took all my love/ And not those things that they were emblems of', just as in 'A Coat' he saw that 'There's more enterprise/ In walking naked'. In 1938, half-way through the two decades of his short poetic life, Thomas too was planning thereafter a more 'naked' craft, in plainer service of the things the poems are 'about'. Especially for such a gregarious young man, the early poems had been strangely unpeopled. Human life was as if submerged by craft and music and image; but the humanity so 'charmingly drowned' will now 'arise to cockcrow and kill' the old poet in him.

We can trace this thread of guilty resolve back earlier. As early as 1934 'Our eunuch dreams' had lamented this displacement of real people by glamorous shadows, in this case the screen images of the craft of cinema. Thomas knew even then that he had to be 'a shouter like the cock,/ Blowing the old dead back' – 'blowing away' mere images and 'breathing life again' into the real people that the images had displaced. But the dilemma was there even further back, at the very beginning of the career. In 'The spire cranes' in 1931, Thomas knew even at the age of seventeen that he had to negotiate between 'the built voice' of craft and the further range of a contingent, prodigal, non-verbal world:

> Those craning birds are choice for you, songs that jump back
> To the built voice, or fly with winter to the bells,
> But do not travel down dumb wind like prodigals.

It will be seen that the poems from around 1938 onwards enter and engage a more recognizably objective, peopled world. Not only with figures like Ann Jones in 'After the funeral' or the poet's son Llewelyn in 'This side of the truth' but with the nameless victims, the shared trauma, of the bombing-raids on London and Swansea, and in the shareable beauty of the landscapes of West Wales. News of the death of the old style was, of course, much exaggerated. No Thomas poem ever really walks naked. The verse-patterns of the later poems are, if anything, even more elaborate. But in terms of theme and subject the later poems do emerge from internal vision, from 'creationist' or 'process' themes, into what Wordsworth called 'the light of common day'.

*

The present volume is a selection of Dylan Thomas's finest poems, representing the full range from the precocious seventeen-year-old in Swansea to the still young poet who died at the age of thirty-nine in New York. The vast majority are from the 1952 *Collected Poems*. In his prefatory note he described that volume as representing 'most of the poems I have written, and all, up to the present year, that I wish to preserve'. As it happens, the first part of that sentence was far from accurate. In selecting the ninety or so poems that constitute the *Collected*

Poems Thomas was, on the contrary, omitting 'most of the poems I have written'. The poetry notebooks of 1930–34 alone contain 164 poems which he was thereby leaving behind. On the other hand, his instinct about what 'I wish to preserve' was irreproachable. He knew very well what was most true to his own vision and voice. He had in any case made the choice five times already in deciding on the contents of the five individual volumes he had published: *18 Poems* (1934), *Twenty-five Poems* (1936), *The Map of Love* (1939), *Deaths and Entrances* (1946) and *In Country Sleep* (1952). He decided to make the *Collected Poems* a simple aggregate of those five volumes, despite the large reservoir of unpublished and published-but-uncollected poems at his disposal. It was a good decision, showing sure judgement as to where he was at his most individual.

The only two poems to disturb that confidence deserve mention, because both are included in this selection. The first is 'Paper and sticks', a poem in *Deaths and Entrances* (1946) which Thomas withdrew from *Collected Poems* at the last moment: he had suddenly had 'the horrors' of it (to E.F. Bozman, 10 September 1952). This was probably because 'Paper and sticks' sounded as if it were in another poet's voice, and closer in any case to Thomas's prose than to his poetry. He arranged for the later major poem 'Do not go gentle into that good night' to be brought forward to take its place. In addition to 'Paper and sticks', the present editor has decided to include in this selection a few other poems, from different periods, to which Thomas did not finally afford 'collected' status. But he did write them and they are, in their own kind, fine poems. They help us gauge what distinguishes the characteristic from the uncharacteristic.

The second poem to break the simple 'aggregate' rule for the contents of the *Collected Poems* in 1952 shows Thomas's decision-process in reverse. 'Once below a time', stylistically a highly characteristic poem, was also intended for *Deaths and Entrances* in 1946 but then withheld because Thomas wanted to do more work on it (the question of craft again – it couldn't be hurried). Six years later he reintroduced it, from the wings as it were, into *Collected Poems*. The stage was set for a volume that, at Thomas's death in 1953, pleased and challenged new audiences and old alike – always uncompromisingly.

*

Finally, a word about the notes. As with introductions or prefaces or paraphrases, in using the notes we should remember the point with which we started – Thomas's strong preference for poems over talk *about* poems. As William York Tindall put it, 'Idea, replacing poem, will drive out marvel.' But marvel will not be lost if we approach the notes through the poems, not vice versa.

It remains true however that, especially in the earlier poems, Thomas is a dense and often difficult poet, and a much more allusive one than has generally been realized. The main aim of the notes to this volume is therefore twofold. First, to offer a broad description of a poem's theme or occasion, not in order to have the poem pinned and wriggling on the wall but to trace the broad outline of its meaning while it is still detached and alive, and to enable the reader to test his or her own view of the general area in which the poem works, whether in agreement or disagreement with the present editor. Second, the notes seek to explain more local points of difficulty or interest. Despite his love of the large crafted shapes of his poems, I don't think Thomas would have objected to my saying that the actual poetry, like the devil, is in the detail, including those 'moments of magical accident' referred to at the beginning. But here again the notes do not aim at uniformity. No two readers would always agree as to what constitutes a problem in the first place, let alone what solves it. The notes therefore do not aim at explaining everything, but at suggesting the range of initial difficulties (of text or context, of syntax or allusion) that the poems might present. The editor hopes that anything thus explained will not be deemed to have been explained away.

Walford Davies

Table of Dates

1914   *27 October:* Dylan Marlais Thomas born 5 Cwmdonkin Drive, Swansea, the son of D. J. Thomas, English Master at Swansea Grammar School. Both parents had their roots in rural Carmarthenshire. A sister, Nancy, had been born 2 September 1906.

1920   Thomas later claims to have started writing poems at the age of six.

1921   Starts at Mrs Hole's School, a 'dame' school in Swansea.

1925   *September:* Enters Swansea Grammar School.
      December: His first poem published in the *Swansea Grammar School Magazine*, to which he regularly contributed poetry and prose, and which he later co-edited.

1927   *14 January:* His first poem to be published nationally: 'His Requiem' in the *Western Mail*.

1929   *3–4 May:* The role of Stanton in the school's production of John Drinkwater's *Abraham Lincoln*, the first of many acting parts that led to his later career as broadcaster.
      10 October: Two lines from a poem submitted by Thomas to a competition are quoted in London's *Everyman* magazine.
      December: His essay on 'Modern Poetry' published in the school magazine.

1930   Sends poems to Robert Graves, who describes them as 'irreproachable'.
      27 April: Starts the first of the four private poetry notebooks, later mined for his published volumes.

1931   *July:* Leaves the Grammar School to become a reporter on the staff of the *South Wales Daily Post* in Swansea. Over the next three years Thomas acts in many productions at the Swansea Little

Theatre – e.g. as Simon Bliss in Coward's *Hay Fever*, Count Bellair in Farquhar's *The Beaux' Stratagem*, and the Host in *The Merry Wives of Windsor*.

1932   *16 December:* Leaves his full-time post with the *South Wales Daily Post*, but continues with freelance journalism, concentrating also on getting his poems published in London. At this time, the first of many visits to London in search of a job.

1933   *March:* 'And death shall have no dominion' published in the *New English Weekly*, Thomas's first London publication.

7 June: Listed as one of twenty-eight winners out of 11,000 contestants in a BBC poetry competition: the poem was read on the BBC National Service, 28 June.

August: Visits London (his married sister lives in a houseboat on the Thames) to place poems with periodicals, notably the *New English Weekly* and the *Adelphi*.

September: 'That Sanity Be Kept', the first of many poems published in the 'Poet's Corner' of Victor Neuberg's *Sunday Referee*. Starts correspondence with Pamela Hansford Johnson.

10 September: Thomas's father admitted to University College Hospital, London, for successful treatment for cancer of the throat.

November: From now on, Thomas also writing short stories, and reviewing for London periodicals.

1934   *14 March:* The publication of 'Light breaks where no sun shines' in the *Listener* prompts inquiries from Stephen Spender and Geoffrey Grigson. Another poet to encourage him at this stage is T. S. Eliot, who later regrets not booking him for Faber.

22 April: 'The force that through the green fuse' wins the 'book prize' of the *Sunday Referee* – the sponsorship of his first volume of poems. Much journeying for the next few years between Swansea and London.

20–22 May: First stay at Laugharne (a Whitsun weekend in the company of Glyn Jones).

20–21 October: Visits (with Glyn Jones) Caradoc Evans at Aberystwyth.

11 November: Moves to London to share rooms with Swansea artist friends Fred Janes and Mervyn Levy.

18 December: 18 Poems (his first volume of poetry) published by the *Sunday Referee* and the Parton Bookshop.

1935   *March:* First meeting (back in Swansea) with Vernon Watkins, immediate friend and major correspondent.

July–August: At Glen Lough, County Donegal (with Geoffrey Grigson).

1936   *8 April:* To Cornwall (Penzance and Mousehole) until 20 May. First meeting with his future wife, Caitlin Macnamara.

11 June: Attends the opening of the International Surrealist Exhibition at the New Burlington Galleries in London.

10 September: Twenty-five Poems published by Dent.

18 December: The poet's father's last day at the Grammar School.

1937   W. H. Auden and Michael Roberts choose 'We lying by seasand' for a special 'English Number' of *Poetry* (Chicago), Thomas's first publication in America.

March: His parents move to Bishopston, outside Swansea.

21 April: Thomas's first broadcast, 'Life and the Modern Poet', starts a long career in broadcasting.

11 July: Marries Caitlin Macnamara at the Register Office in Penzance.

1 September: Leaves Cornwall to stay at his parents' new home outside Swansea.

1 October: Moves to his mother-in-law's house at Blashford in Hampshire.

1938   *January:* Writes to Henry Treece, supporting the book Treece is planning on his poetry.

March: First negotiations (with James Laughlin) for American publication of his work.

April: Moves from Blashford to his parents' house outside Swansea, and then (May) to Laugharne. Along with London, these were his main homes for the next three years.

November: Poetry (Chicago) awards him its Oscar Blumenthal Prize.

1939   *30 January:* First child, Llewelyn, born in the hospital at Poole, Dorset.

24 August: The Map of Love (poetry and prose) published by Dent.

3 September: Second World War declared.

20 December: The World I Breathe, a selection of Thomas's poetry and prose, published by New Directions in New York – his first volume publication in America.

1940 *4 April: Portrait of the Artist as a Young Dog* (autobiographical short stories) published by Dent.

6 April: Registers for military service, but later turned down on medical grounds.

4 July: Moves with other artists to John Davenport's house at Marshfield in Gloucestershire. Until November, collaborates with Davenport on a parodic novel, *The Death of the King's Canary*.

24 September: American edition of *Portrait of the Artist as a Young Dog* published.

1941 *22–24 February:* Incendiary bombs devastate Swansea.

April: Decides to sell the poetry notebooks and other material. The last poem taken from the notebooks for publication is 'The Hunchback in the Park'.

October: Starts as script-writer for Strand Films.

1942 *20 August:* Joins Caitlin in Talsarn, Cardiganshire. The start of a period in different parts of West Wales that in 1944–5 saw a burst of new writing in the otherwise lean years of the war.

1943 *7 January:* Records 'Reminiscences of Childhood' for BBC Welsh Home Service.

25 January: New Poems published by New Directions in New York.

3 March: Daughter, Aeronwy, born in London, but named after the Aeron river in Cardiganshire.

September: The family joins Thomas's parents at Llangain, near the now famous farm Fernhill (subject of the poem 'Fern Hill').

1944 *February:* Family moves to a cottage near Bosham in Sussex to avoid the London bombing raids, but still retains a flat in Chelsea.

June: After the closure of Strand Films, Thomas kept on at Gryphon Films. He later writes also for Stratford Film and Gainsborough Films.

6 June: D-Day.

4 September: Family moves to New Quay, a small fishing village on Cardigan Bay – along with Laugharne, the main inspiration for the setting of *Under Milk Wood*.

14 December: Records in London 'Quite Early One Morning' (a direct precursor of *Under Milk Wood*) for later transmission by the BBC Welsh Home Service.

1945   *8 May:* VE Day.

July: Leaves New Quay.

15 August: VJ Day.

6 December: Records 'Memories of Christmas' for the BBC Welsh Service Children's Hour.

1946   From early 1946 to May 1949 living in or near Oxford.

7 February: Deaths and Entrances (poems) published by Dent.

24 March: Signs, at T. S. Eliot's request, a letter in support of Ezra Pound.

13 May: Reads 'Fern Hill', Lawrence's 'Snake' and Blake's 'Tyger' in the Command Performance for the Queen at Wigmore Hall.

8 November: Selected Writings published by New Directions in New York.

1947   *10–12 February:* Revisits Swansea to collect information for the broadcast 'Return Journey'.

April–August: A family visit, via Calais, Switzerland and Milan, to Rapallo, funded by a Society of Authors award on Edith Sitwell's recommendation – her way of saving him from having to go to America.

12 August: Settles at South Leigh, near Witney, Oxfordshire.

1948   *February:* Thomas at Llangain looking after his father, while his mother is in hospital.

21 April: Rents a cottage at South Leigh for his parents, who are both ill.

1949   *4–9 March:* Attends an artists' conference in Prague at the invitation of the Czech cultural attaché in London.

May: The family moves to the Boat House at Laugharne.

28 May: Receives and accepts the first invitation by John Malcolm Brinnin, Director of the Poetry Center in New York City, to visit America on a lecture tour.

24 July: Son, Colm, born in Carmarthen Hospital.

6 August: Contributes first piece ('Over Sir John's hill') to Marguerite Caetani's magazine *Botteghe Oscure* in Rome, soon also to receive poems like 'Lament' and 'Do not go gentle into that good night', and the first published version of a part of *Under Milk Wood*.

1950   *20 February:* Flies to New York on his first American tour, returning 31 May on the liner *Queen Elizabeth*, after around forty public readings. This hectic schedule remains the pattern for another three American tours.

1–6 September: John Malcolm Brinnin visits Thomas at Laugharne.

1951   *8 January–14 February:* In Persia to write a documentary filmscript for the Anglo-Iranian Oil Company.

1952   *15 January:* Thomas and Caitlin embark on the *Queen Mary* for the second American tour, returning on the *New Amsterdam* four months later.

February: In Country Sleep (poems) published in America only.

9 October: Agrees to J. Alexander Rolph's compiling a bibliography of his works.

10 November: Collected Poems 1934–1952 published by Dent, selling 30,000 copies of the English edition alone.

16 December: Thomas's father dies, aged seventy-six.

1953   *20 January:* Receives the William Foyle Poetry Prize for 1952.

31 March: American edition of *Collected Poems 1934–1952* published by New Directions in New York.

16 April: On the SS *United States* en route for his third American tour. Death of his sister Nancy in India.

14 May: Under Milk Wood's first performance at the Poetry Center in New York. *The Doctor and the Devils* becomes the first of the filmscripts to be published.

23 May: Discusses with Stravinsky in Boston collaboration for an opera.

3 June: Flies home, the day after the coronation of Queen Elizabeth II.

5 October: Reads part of *Under Milk Wood* at the Tenby Arts Club.

8 October: The film script *The Doctor and the Devils* published by New Directions in New York.

9 October: Leaves Laugharne en route, via Swansea, for his flight on the 19th for his final American tour. Delivers *Under Milk Wood* to the BBC for typing.

20 October: Though ill, Thomas commits himself in rehearsals of *Under Milk Wood* for performances at the Poetry Center in New York on the 24th and 25th, and to a symposium at City College, New York, on 'Film Art' (in a group including Arthur Miller) on the 28th.

27 October: Thomas's thirty-ninth birthday.

4 November: Ill and in pain, injected with an overdose of morphine by a New York doctor. Falls into a coma.

7 November: Caitlin Thomas flies to New York.

9 November: Dies at St Vincent's Hospital, New York City.

24 November: Buried at St Martin's Church in Laugharne.

1982   *1 March:* Memorial stone laid in Poets' Corner, Westminster Abbey.

Further Reading

EDITIONS

Thomas, Dylan, *Collected Stories*, ed. Walford Davies, introduced by Leslie Norris, Dent, 1983.

—— *Collected Poems 1934–1953*, ed. Walford Davies and Ralph Maud, Dent, 1988.

—— *The Notebook Poems 1930–1934*, ed. Ralph Maud, Dent, 1989.

—— *The Broadcasts*, ed. Ralph Maud, Dent, 1991.

—— *Selected Poems*, ed. Walford Davies, Dent, 1993.

—— *The Filmscripts*, ed. John Ackerman, Dent, 1995.

—— *The Dylan Thomas Omnibus*, Dent, 1995. Incorporating Thomas's poems, stories and broadcasts, including *Under Milk Wood*.

—— *Under Milk Wood*, ed. Walford Davies and Ralph Maud, Dent, 1995.

—— *Under Milk Wood*, ed. Walford Davies, Penguin, 2000.

RECORDINGS

Dylan Thomas Reading his Complete Recorded Poetry, Caedmon Publishers, LP recording TC 2014, New York, 1963.

Under Milk Wood, Caedmon Publishers, LP recording TC 2005, New York, 1954. A recording of the first completed text in a stage reading at the Poetry Center of New York's Young Men's and Young Women's Hebrew Association, 14 May 1953. Directed by Dylan Thomas, who participated as First Voice and as the Reverend Eli Jenkins.

BIOGRAPHY

Brinnin, John Malcolm, *Dylan Thomas in America*, Dent, 1956.

Davies, James A., *Dylan Thomas's Places: A Biographical and Literary Guide*, Christopher Davies, 1987.

Ferris, Paul, *Caitlin: The Life of Caitlin Thomas*, Hutchinson, 1993.

—— *Dylan Thomas: The Biography*, New Edition, Dent, 1999. The standard biography of 1977, revised and updated.

FitzGibbon, Constantine, *The Life of Dylan Thomas*, Dent, 1965.

Johnson, Pamela Hansford, *Important to Me: Personalia*, Macmillan, 1974.

Jones, Daniel, *My Friend Dylan Thomas*, Dent, 1977.

McKenna, Rollie, *Portrait of Dylan: A Photographer's Memoir* (with an introduction by John Malcolm Brinnin), Dent, 1982.

Read, Bill, *The Days of Dylan Thoms*, Weidenfeld and Nicolson, 1964.

Sinclair, Andrew, *Dylan Thomas: Poet of His People*, Michael Joseph, 1975.

Thomas, Caitlin, *Leftover Life to Kill*, Putnam, 1957.

Thomas, Caitlin, with George Tremlett, *Caitlin: A Warring Absence*, Secker & Warburg, 1986.

Tremlett, George, *Dylan Thomas: In the Mercy of His Means*, Constable 1991.

Watkins, Gwen, *Portrait of a Friend*, Gomer, 1983.

LETTERS

Dylan Thomas: Letters to Vernon Watkins, ed. Vernon Watkins, Dent and Faber & Faber, 1957.

Dylan Thomas: Collected Letters, ed. Paul Ferris, Dent, 2000. The authoritative *Collected Letters* of 1985 enlarged and updated.

BIBLIOGRAPHY

Gaston, Georg M. A., *Dylan Thomas: A Reference Guide*, G. K. Hall, 1987.

Harris, John, *A Bibliographical Guide to Twenty-four Modern Anglo-Welsh Writers*, University of Wales Press, 1994.

—— Updating bibliographies of Dylan Thomas, along with other Anglo-Welsh writers, in *Welsh Writing in English: A Yearbook of Critical Essays*, ed. Tony Brown, New Welsh Review, 1995 onwards.

Maud, Ralph, *Dylan Thomas in Print: A Bibliographical History* (with an appendix by Walford Davies), Dent, 1972. The standard bibliography.

Rolph, J. Alexander, *Dylan Thomas: A Bibliography*, Dent, 1956.

CRITICAL AND OTHER STUDIES

Ackerman, John, *Dylan Thomas: His Life and Work*, Macmillan, 1991.

—— *Welsh Dylan*, Seren, 1998.

—— *A Dylan Thomas Companion: Life, Poetry and Prose*, Macmillan, 1991.

Bayley, John, *The Romantic Survival*, Constable, 1957.

Bold, Alan (ed.), *Dylan Thomas: Craft or Sullen Art*, Vision Press, 1990.

Brooke-Rose, Christine, *A Grammar of Metaphor*, Secker & Warburg, 1958.

Conran, Anthony, *The Cost of Strangeness*, Gomer, 1982.

Cox, C. B. (ed.), *Dylan Thomas: A Collection of Critical Essays*, 'Twentieth Century Views' series, Prentice-Hall, 1966.

—— 'Welsh Bards in Hard Times: Dylan Thomas and R. S. Thomas', in vol. 8 ('The Present') of *The New Pelican Guide to English Literature*, ed. Boris Ford, Penguin, 1983.

Davies, Aneirin Talfan, *Dylan: Druid of the Broken Body*, Dent, 1964.

Davies, James A., *A Reference Companion to Dylan Thomas*, Greenwood Press, 1998.

—— 'A Picnic in the Orchard: Dylan Thomas's Wales', in *Wales: the Imagined Nation*, ed. Tony Curtis, Poetry Wales Press, 1986.

Davies, Walford, *Dylan Thomas*, 'Writers of Wales' series, University of Wales Press, 1990.

—— (ed.) *Dylan Thomas: New Critical Essays*, Dent, 1972.

—— *Dylan Thomas*, 'Open Guides' series, Open University Press, 1986.

—— *Dylan Thomas: The Poet in His Chains*, the W. D. Thomas Memorial Lecture, the University of Wales, Swansea, 1986.

—— 'Bright Fields, Loud Hills, and the Glimpsed Good Place: R. S.

Thomas and Dylan Thomas', in *The Page's Drift*, ed. M. Wynn Thomas, Seren, 1993.

Emery, Clark, *The World of Dylan Thomas*, University of Miami Press, 1962.

Grindea, Miron (ed.), *Adam International Review: Dylan Thomas Memorial Number*, Year XXI, No. 238, 1953.

Hardy, Barbara, *The Advantage of Lyric: Essays on Feeling in Poetry*, Athlone Press, 1977.

—— *Dylan Thomas's Poetic Language: The Stream that is Flowing Both Ways*, the Gwyn Jones Lecture, the University of Wales, Cardiff, 1987.

—— 'Region and Nation: R. S. Thomas and Dylan Thomas', in *The Literature of Region and Nation*, ed. R. P. Draper, Macmillan, 1989.

Heaney, Seamus, 'Dylan the Durable? On Dylan Thomas', in *The Redress of Poetry*, Faber, 1995.

Holbrook, David, 'Two Welsh Writers: T. F. Powys and Dylan Thomas', in *The Pelican Guide to English Literature: The Modern Age*, ed. Boris Ford, Penguin Books, 1961.

—— *Llareggub Revisited: Dylan Thomas and the State of Modern Poetry*, Bowes & Bowes, 1962.

—— *Dylan Thomas: The Code of Night*, Athlone Press, 1972.

Jones, Glyn, *The Dragon Has Two Tongues*, Dent, 1968.

Jones, T. H., *Dylan Thomas*, Oliver & Boyd, 1963.

Kershner, R. B., Jr., *Dylan Thomas: The Poet and His Critics*, American Library Association, 1976.

Kleinman, H. H., *The Religious Sonnets of Dylan Thomas*, University of California Press, 1963.

Korg, Jacob, *Dylan Thomas*, 'Twayne's English Authors' series, Twayne, 1965.

Mathias, Roland, *A Ride Through the Wood*, Poetry Wales Press, 1985.

Maud, Ralph, *Entrances to Dylan Thomas' Poetry*, University of Pittsburgh Press, 1963.

—— and Davies, Aneirin Talfan (eds.), *The Colour of Saying: An Anthology of Verse Spoken by Dylan Thomas*, Dent, 1963.

—— (ed.), *Wales in His Arms: Dylan Thomas's Choice of Welsh Poetry*, University of Wales Press, 1994.

Mayer, Ann Elizabeth, *Artists in Dylan Thomas's Prose Works*, McGill–Queen's University Press, 1995.

Miller, J. Hillis, *Poets of Reality: Six Twentieth Century Writers*, Harvard University Press, 1966.

Morrison, Blake, *The Movement; English Poetry and Fiction of the 1950s*, Methuen, 1986.

Moynihan, William T., *The Craft and Art of Dylan Thomas*, Cornell University Press, 1968.

Nowottny, Winifred, *The Language Poets Use*, Athlone Press, 1962.

Olson, Elder, *The Poetry of Dylan Thomas*, University of Chicago Press, 1954.

Pratt, Annis, *Dylan Thomas' Early Prose: A Study in Creative Mythology*, University of Pittsburgh Press, 1970.

Peach, Linden, *The Prose Writing of Dylan Thomas*, Macmillan, 1988.

Rawson, Claude, 'Dylan Thomas', in *Talks to Teachers of English 2*, Department of Education, King's College, Newcastle, 1962.

Stanford, Derek, *Dylan Thomas*, Citadel Press, 1964.

Tedlock, E. W. (ed.), *Dylan Thomas: The Legend and the Poet*, Heinemann, 1960.

Tindall, William York, *A Reader's Guide to Dylan Thomas*, Octagon Books, 1981.

Treece, Henry, *Dylan Thomas: 'Dog Among the Fairies'*, Ernest Benn, 1956.

A Note on the Text

The great majority of the poems in this selection are from within Dylan Thomas's own choice for his *Collected Poems 1934–1952*, published by J. M. Dent & Sons in 1952 and representing all the poems that Thomas at that time wished to preserve. This was a year before his death in New York City on 9 November 1953. In 1988 Dent published an edition of the *Collected* volume edited by Walford Davies and Ralph Maud as *Collected Poems 1934–1953*. (The extension to 1953 was so as to include reconstructions of two unfinished poems – 'Elegy' and 'In Country Heaven' – that Thomas was working on towards the end of his life.) The Davies/Maud volume made a wide range of emendations to the 1952 text, and is now the standard edition. The text of the great majority of the poems in the present selection is from that volume, embracing minor corrections made in its eleven reprintings since 1988.

The textual sources of the other poems chosen are as follows: 'Their faces shone under some radiance' (*The Notebook Poems 1930–1934*, ed. Ralph Maud, Dent, 1989); 'That sanity be kept' (*Sunday Referee*, 3 September 1933); 'The Countryman's Return' (*The Cambridge Front*, no. 1, summer 1940); 'An old man or a young man' (a manuscript quoted by permission of the Harry Ransom Humanities Research Center of the University of Texas); Eli Jenkins's morning poem and the stanzas between Captain Cat and Rosie Probert (*Under Milk Wood*, ed. Walford Davies and Ralph Maud, Dent, 1995).

In consonance with what seems to have been Thomas's preference in 1952, all titles that are, partially or completely, the first line of a poem are printed exactly as in that opening line.

The Poems

1 Prologue

This day winding down now
At God speeded summer's end
In the torrent salmon sun,
In my seashaken house
On a breakneck of rocks
Tangled with chirrup and fruit,
Froth, flute, fin and quill
At a wood's dancing hoof,
By scummed, starfish sands
With their fishwife cross
Gulls, pipers, cockles, and sails,
Out there, crow black, men
Tackled with clouds, who kneel
To the sunset nets,
Geese nearly in heaven, boys
Stabbing, and herons, and shells
That speak seven seas,
Eternal waters away
From the cities of nine
Days' night whose towers will catch
In the religious wind
Like stalks of tall, dry straw,
At poor peace I sing
To you, strangers, (though song
Is a burning and crested act,
The fire of birds in
The world's turning wood,
For my sawn, splay sounds),
Out of these seathumbed leaves
That will fly and fall
Like leaves of trees and as soon

Crumble and undie
Into the dogdayed night.
Seaward the salmon, sucked sun slips,
35   And the dumb swans drub blue
My dabbed bay's dusk, as I hack
This rumpus of shapes
For you to know
How I, a spinning man,
40   Glory also this star, bird
Roared, sea born, man torn, blood blest.
Hark: I trumpet the place,
From fish to jumping hill! Look:
I build my bellowing ark
45   To the best of my love
As the flood begins,
Out of the fountainhead
Of fear, rage red, manalive,
Molten and mountainous to stream
50   Over the wound asleep
Sheep white hollow farms

To Wales in my arms.
Hoo, there, in castle keep,
You king singsong owls, who moonbeam
55   The flickering runs and dive
The dingle furred deer dead!
Huloo, on plumbed bryns,
O my ruffled ring dove
In the hooting, nearly dark
60   With Welsh and reverent rook,
Coo rooing the woods' praise,
Who moons her blue notes from her nest
Down to the curlew herd!
Ho, hullaballoing clan
65   Agape, with woe
In your beaks, on the gabbing capes!

Heigh, on horseback hill, jack
Whisking hare! who
Hears, there, this fox light, my flood ship's
70 Clangour as I hew and smite
(A clash of anvils for my
Hubbub and fiddle, this tune
On a tongued puffball)
But animals thick as thieves
75 On God's rough tumbling grounds
(Hail to His beasthood!).
Beasts who sleep good and thin,
Hist, in hogsback woods! The haystacked
Hollow farms in a throng
80 Of waters cluck and cling,
And barnroofs cockcrow war!
O kingdom of neighbours, finned
Felled and quilled, flash to my patch
Work ark and the moonshine
85 Drinking Noah of the bay,
With pelt, and scale, and fleece:
Only the drowned deep bells
Of sheep and churches noise
Poor peace as the sun sets
90 And dark shoals every holy field.
We shall ride out alone, and then,
Under the stars of Wales,
Cry, Multitudes of arks! Across
The water lidded lands,
95 Manned with their loves they'll move,
Like wooden islands, hill to hill.
Huloo, my prowed dove with a flute!
Ahoy, old, sea-legged fox,
Tom tit and Dai mouse!
100 My ark sings in the sun
At God speeded summer's end
And the flood flowers now.

2 *The spire cranes*

The spire cranes. Its statue is an aviary.
From the stone nest it does not let the feathery
Carved birds blunt their striking throats on the salt gravel,
Pierce the spilt sky with diving wing in weed and heel
5   An inch in froth. Chimes cheat the prison spire, pelter
In time like outlaw rains on that priest, water,
Time for the swimmers' hands, music for silver lock
And mouth. Both note and plume plunge from the spire's hook.
Those craning birds are choice for you, songs that jump back
10   To the built voice, or fly with winter to the bells,
But do not travel down dumb wind like prodigals.

3 *Out of the sighs*

Out of the sighs a little comes,
But not of grief, for I have knocked down that
Before the agony; the spirit grows,
Forgets, and cries;
5   A little comes, is tasted and found good;
All could not disappoint;
There must, be praised, some certainty,
If not of loving well, then not,
And that is true after perpetual defeat.

10   After such fighting as the weakest know,
There's more than dying;
Lose the great pains or stuff the wound,
He'll ache too long
Through no regret of leaving woman waiting
15   For her soldier stained with spilt words
That spill such acrid blood.

Were that enough, enough to ease the pain,
Feeling regret when this is wasted
That made me happy in the sun,
20   And, sleeping, made me dream
How much was happy while it lasted,
Were vaguenesses enough and the sweet lies plenty,
The hollow words could bear all suffering
And cure me of ills.

25   Were that enough, bone, blood, and sinew,
The twisted brain, the fair-formed loin,
Groping for matter under the dog's plate,
Man should be cured of distemper.
For all there is to give I offer:
30   Crumbs, barn, and halter.

4 *Their faces shone under some radiance*

Their faces shone under some radiance
Of mingled moonlight and lamplight
That turned the empty kisses into meaning,
The island of such penny love
5   Into a costly country, the graves
That neighboured them to wells of warmth
(And skeletons had sap). One minute
Their faces shone; the midnight rain
Hung pointed in the wind,
10   Before the moon shifted and the sap ran out,
She, in her summer frock, saying some cheap thing,
And he replying,
Not knowing radiance came and passed.
The suicides parade again, now ripe for dying.

5   *I have longed to move away*

I have longed to move away
From the hissing of the spent lie
And the old terrors' continual cry
Growing more terrible as the day
Goes over the hill into the deep sea;
I have longed to move away
From the repetition of salutes,
For there are ghosts in the air
And ghostly echoes on paper,
And the thunder of calls and notes.

I have longed to move away but am afraid;
Some life, yet unspent, might explode
Out of the old lie burning on the ground,
And, crackling into the air, leave me half-blind.
Neither by night's ancient fear,
The parting of hat from hair,
Pursed lips at the receiver,
Shall I fall to death's feather.
By these I would not care to die,
Half convention and half lie.

6   *And death shall have no dominion*

And death shall have no dominion.
Dead men naked they shall be one
With the man in the wind and the west moon;
When their bones are picked clean and the clean bones gone,
They shall have stars at elbow and foot;
Though they go mad they shall be sane,

Though they sink through the sea they shall rise again;
Though lovers be lost love shall not;
And death shall have no dominion.

10   And death shall have no dominion.
Under the windings of the sea
They lying long shall not die windily;
Twisting on racks when sinews give way,
Strapped to a wheel, yet they shall not break;
15   Faith in their hands shall snap in two,
And the unicorn evils run them through;
Split all ends up they shan't crack;
And death shall have no dominion.

And death shall have no dominion.
20   No more may gulls cry at their ears
Or waves break loud on the seashores;
Where blew a flower may a flower no more
Lift its head to the blows of the rain;
Though they be mad and dead as nails,
25   Heads of the characters hammer through daisies;
Break in the sun till the sun breaks down,
And death shall have no dominion.

7 *We lying by seasand*

We lying by seasand, watching yellow
And the grave sea, mock who deride
Who follow the red rivers, hollow
Alcove of words out of cicada shade,
5   For in this yellow grave of sand and sea
A calling for colour calls with the wind
That's grave and gay as grave and sea

Sleeping on either hand.
The lunar silences, the silent tide
10   Lapping the still canals, the dry tide-master
Ribbed between desert and water storm,
Should cure our ills of the water
With a one-coloured calm;
The heavenly music over the sand
15   Sounds with the grains as they hurry
Hiding the golden mountains and mansions
Of the grave, gay, seaside land.
Bound by a sovereign strip, we lie,
Watch yellow, wish for wind to blow away
20   The strata of the shore and drown red rock;
But wishes breed not, neither
Can we fend off rock arrival,
Lie watching yellow until the golden weather
Breaks, O my heart's blood, like a heart and hill.

8 *Find meat on bones*

'Find meat on bones that soon have none,
And drink in the two milked crags,
The merriest marrow and the dregs
Before the ladies' breasts are hags
5   And the limbs are torn.
Disturb no winding-sheets, my son,
But when the ladies are cold as stone
Then hang a ram rose over the rags.

Rebel against the binding moon
10   And the parliament of sky,
The kingcrafts of the wicked sea,
Autocracy of night and day,
Dictatorship of sun.

Rebel against the flesh and bone,
15   The word of the blood, the wily skin,
And the maggot no man can slay.'

'The thirst is quenched, the hunger gone,
And my heart is cracked across;
My face is haggard in the glass,
20   My lips are withered with a kiss,
My breasts are thin.
A merry girl took me for man,
I laid her down and told her sin,
And put beside her a ram rose.

25   The maggot that no man can kill
And the man no rope can hang
Rebel against my father's dream
That out of a bower of red swine
Howls the foul fiend to heel.
30   I cannot murder, like a fool,
Season and sunshine, grace and girl,
Nor can I smother the sweet waking.

Black night still ministers the moon,
And the sky lays down her laws,
35   The sea speaks in a kingly voice,
Light and dark are no enemies
But one companion.
"War on the spider and the wren!
War on the destiny of man!
40   Doom on the sun!"
Before death takes you, O take back this.'

9 *Ears in the turrets hear*

Ears in the turrets hear
Hands grumble on the door,
Eyes in the gables see
The fingers at the locks.
5   Shall I unbolt or stay
Alone till the day I die
Unseen by stranger-eyes
In this white house?
Hands, hold you poison or grapes?

10 Beyond this island bound
By a thin sea of flesh
And a bone coast,
The land lies out of sound
And the hills out of mind.
15 No bird or flying fish
Disturbs this island's rest.

Ears in this island hear
The wind pass like a fire,
Eyes in this island see
20 Ships anchor off the bay.
Shall I run to the ships
With the wind in my hair,
Or stay till the day I die
And welcome no sailor?
25 Ships, hold you poison or grapes?

Hands grumble on the door,
Ships anchor off the bay,
Rain beats the sand and slates.

Shall I let in the stranger,
Shall I welcome the sailor,
Or stay till the day I die?

Hands of the stranger and holds of the ships,
Hold you poison or grapes?

10   *Why east wind chills*

Why east wind chills and south wind cools
Shall not be known till windwell dries
And west's no longer drowned
In winds that bring the fruit and rind
Of many a hundred falls;
Why silk is soft and the stone wounds
The child shall question all his days,
Why night-time rain and the breast's blood
Both quench his thirst he'll have a black reply.

When cometh Jack Frost? the children ask.
Shall they clasp a comet in their fists?
Not till, from high and low, their dust
Sprinkles in children's eyes a long-last sleep
And dusk is crowded with the children's ghosts,
Shall a white answer echo from the rooftops.

All things are known: the stars' advice
Calls some content to travel with the winds,
Though what the stars ask as they round
Time upon time the towers of the skies
Is heard but little till the stars go out.

I hear content, and 'Be content'
Ring like a handbell through the corridors,
And 'Know no answer,' and I know
No answer to the children's cry
Of echo's answer and the man of frost
And ghostly comets over the raised fists.

25

11 The hand that signed the paper

The hand that signed the paper felled a city;
Five sovereign fingers taxed the breath,
Doubled the globe of dead and halved a country;
These five kings did a king to death.

5 The mighty hand leads to a sloping shoulder,
The finger joints are cramped with chalk;
A goose's quill has put an end to murder
That put an end to talk.

The hand that signed the treaty bred a fever,
10 And famine grew, and locusts came;
Great is the hand that holds dominion over
Man by a scribbled name.

The five kings count the dead, but do not soften
The crusted wound nor stroke the brow;
15 A hand rules pity as a hand rules heaven;
Hands have no tears to flow.

12 *That sanity be kept*

That sanity be kept I sit at open windows,
Regard the sky, make unobtrusive comment on the moon,
Sit at open windows in my shirt,
And let the traffic pass, the signals shine,
The engines run, the brass bands keep in tune,
For sanity must be preserved.

Thinking of death, I sit and watch the park
Where children play in all their innocence,
And matrons, on the littered grass,
Absorb the daily sun.

The sweet suburban music from a hundred lawns
Comes softly to my ears. The English mowers mow and mow.

I mark the couples walking arm in arm,
Observe their smiles,
Sweet invitations and inventions,
See them lend love illustration
By gesture and grimace.
I watch them curiously, detect beneath the laughs
What stands for grief, a vague bewilderment
At things not turning right.

I sit at open windows in my shirt,
Observe, like some Jehovah of the west,
What passes by, that sanity be kept.

13 Before I knocked

Before I knocked and flesh let enter,
With liquid hands tapped on the womb,
I who was shapeless as the water
That shaped the Jordan near my home
Was brother to Mnetha's daughter
And sister to the fathering worm.

I who was deaf to spring and summer,
Who knew not sun nor moon by name,
Felt thud beneath my flesh's armour,
As yet was in a molten form,
The leaden stars, the rainy hammer
Swung by my father from his dome.

I knew the message of the winter,
The darted hail, the childish snow,
And the wind was my sister suitor;
Wind in me leaped, the hellborn dew;
My veins flowed with the Eastern weather;
Ungotten I knew night and day.

As yet ungotten, I did suffer,
The rack of dreams my lily bones
Did twist into a living cipher,
And flesh was snipped to cross the lines
Of gallow crosses on the liver
And brambles in the wringing brains.

My throat knew thirst before the structure
Of skin and vein around the well
Where words and water make a mixture

Unfailing till the blood runs foul;
My heart knew love, my belly hunger;
30   I smelt the maggot in my stool.

And time cast forth my mortal creature
To drift or drown upon the seas
Acquainted with the salt adventure
Of tides that never touch the shores.
35   I who was rich was made the richer
By sipping at the vine of days.

I, born of flesh and ghost, was neither
A ghost nor man, but mortal ghost.
And I was struck down by death's feather.
40   I was mortal to the last
Long breath that carried to my father
The message of his dying christ.

You who bow down at cross and altar,
Remember me and pity Him
45   Who took my flesh and bone for armour
And doublecrossed my mother's womb.

14 *My hero bares his nerves*

My hero bares his nerves along my wrist
That rules from wrist to shoulder,
Unpacks the head that, like a sleepy ghost,
Leans on my mortal ruler,
5   The proud spine spurning turn and twist.

And these poor nerves so wired to the skull
Ache on the lovelorn paper
I hug to love with my unruly scrawl
That utters all love hunger
10   And tells the page the empty ill.

My hero bares my side and sees his heart
Tread, like a naked Venus,
The beach of flesh, and wind her bloodred plait;
Stripping my loin of promise,
15   He promises a secret heat.

He holds the wire from this box of nerves
Praising the mortal error
Of birth and death, the two sad knaves of thieves,
And the hunger's emperor;
20   He pulls the chain, the cistern moves.

15 *The force that through the green fuse*

The force that through the green fuse drives the flower
Drives my green age; that blasts the roots of trees
Is my destroyer.
And I am dumb to tell the crooked rose
5   My youth is bent by the same wintry fever.

The force that drives the water through the rocks
Drives my red blood; that dries the mouthing streams
Turns mine to wax.
And I am dumb to mouth unto my veins
10   How at the mountain spring the same mouth sucks.

The hand that whirls the water in the pool
Stirs the quicksand; that ropes the blowing wind
Hauls my shroud sail.
And I am dumb to tell the hanging man
How of my clay is made the hangman's lime.

The lips of time leech to the fountain head;
Love drips and gathers, but the fallen blood
Shall calm her sores.
And I am dumb to tell a weather's wind
How time has ticked a heaven round the stars.

And I am dumb to tell the lover's tomb
How at my sheet goes the same crooked worm.

16   *In the beginning*

In the beginning was the three-pointed star,
One smile of light across the empty face;
One bough of bone across the rooting air,
The substance forked that marrowed the first sun;
And, burning ciphers on the round of space,
Heaven and hell mixed as they spun.

In the beginning was the pale signature,
Three-syllabled and starry as the smile;
And after came the imprints on the water,
Stamp of the minted face upon the moon;
The blood that touched the crosstree and the grail
Touched the first cloud and left a sign.

In the beginning was the mounting fire
That set alight the weathers from a spark,
A three-eyed, red-eyed spark, blunt as a flower;

Life rose and spouted from the rolling seas,
Burst in the roots, pumped from the earth and rock
The secret oils that drive the grass.

In the beginning was the word, the word
20   That from the solid bases of the light
Abstracted all the letters of the void;
And from the cloudy bases of the breath
The word flowed up, translating to the heart
First character of birth and death.

25   In the beginning was the secret brain.
The brain was celled and soldered in the thought
Before the pitch was forking to a sun;
Before the veins were shaking in their sieve,
Blood shot and scattered to the winds of light
30   The ribbed original of love.

17 Light breaks where no sun shines

Light breaks where no sun shines;
Where no sea runs, the waters of the heart
Push in their tides;
And, broken ghosts with glow-worms in their heads,
5   The things of light
File through the flesh where no flesh decks the bones.

A candle in the thighs
Warms youth and seed and burns the seeds of age;
Where no seed stirs,
10   The fruit of man unwrinkles in the stars,
Bright as a fig;
Where no wax is, the candle shows its hairs.

Dawn breaks behind the eyes;
From poles of skull and toe the windy blood
15   Slides like a sea;
Nor fenced, nor staked, the gushers of the sky
Spout to the rod
Divining in a smile the oil of tears.

Night in the sockets rounds,
20   Like some pitch moon, the limit of the globes;
Day lights the bone;
Where no cold is, the skinning gales unpin
The winter's robes;
The film of spring is hanging from the lids.

25   Light breaks on secret lots,
On tips of thought where thoughts smell in the rain;
When logics die,
The secret of the soil grows through the eye,
And blood jumps in the sun;
30   Above the waste allotments the dawn halts.

18 This bread I break

This bread I break was once the oat,
This wine upon a foreign tree
Plunged in its fruit;
Man in the day or wind at night
5   Laid the crops low, broke the grape's joy.

Once in this wine the summer blood
Knocked in the flesh that decked the vine,
Once in this bread
The oat was merry in the wind;
10   Man broke the sun, pulled the wind down.

This flesh you break, this blood you let
Make desolation in the vein,
Were oat and grape
Born of the sensual root and sap;
15   My wine you drink, my bread you snap.

19   When once the twilight locks

When once the twilight locks no longer
Locked in the long worm of my finger
Nor dammed the sea that sped about my fist,
The mouth of time sucked, like a sponge,
5   The milky acid on each hinge,
And swallowed dry the waters of the breast.

When the galactic sea was sucked
And all the dry seabed unlocked,
I sent my creature scouting on the globe,
10   That globe itself of hair and bone
That, sewn to me by nerve and brain,
Had stringed my flask of matter to his rib.

My fuses timed to charge his heart,
He blew like powder to the light
15   And held a little sabbath with the sun,
But when the stars, assuming shape,
Drew in his eyes the straws of sleep,
He drowned his father's magics in a dream.

All issue armoured, of the grave,
20   The redhaired cancer still alive,
The cataracted eyes that filmed their cloth;

Some dead undid their bushy jaws,
And bags of blood let out their flies;
He had by heart the Christ-cross-row of death.

25 Sleep navigates the tides of time;
The dry Sargasso of the tomb
Gives up its dead to such a working sea;
And sleep rolls mute above the beds
Where fishes' food is fed the shades
30 Who periscope through flowers to the sky.

The hanged who lever from the limes
Ghostly propellers for their limbs,
The cypress lads who wither with the cock,
These, and the others in sleep's acres,
35 Of dreaming men make moony suckers,
And snipe the fools of vision in the back.

When once the twilight screws were turned,
And mother milk was stiff as sand,
I sent my own ambassador to light;
40 By trick or chance he fell asleep
And conjured up a carcase shape
To rob me of my fluids in his heart.

Awake, my sleeper, to the sun,
A worker in the morning town,
45 And leave the poppied pickthank where he lies;
The fences of the light are down,
All but the briskest riders thrown,
And worlds hang on the trees.

20 *A process in the weather of the heart*

A process in the weather of the heart
Turns damp to dry; the golden shot
Storms in the freezing tomb.
A weather in the quarter of the veins
Turns night to day; blood in their suns
Lights up the living worm.

A process in the eye forwarns
The bones of blindness; and the womb
Drives in a death as life leaks out.

A darkness in the weather of the eye
Is half its light; the fathomed sea
Breaks on unangled land.
The seed that makes a forest of the loin
Forks half its fruit; and half drops down,
Slow in a sleeping wind.

A weather in the flesh and bone
Is damp and dry; the quick and dead
Move like two ghosts before the eye.

A process in the weather of the world
Turns ghost to ghost; each mothered child
Sits in their double shade.
A process blows the moon into the sun,
Pulls down the shabby curtains of the skin;
And the heart gives up its dead.

21   *Foster the light*

Foster the light nor veil the manshaped moon,
Nor weather winds that blow not down the bone,
But strip the twelve-winded marrow from his circle;
Master the night nor serve the snowman's brain
5 That shapes each bushy item of the air
Into a polestar pointed on an icicle.

Murmur of spring nor crush the cockerel's eggs,
Nor hammer back a season in the figs,
But graft these four-fruited ridings on your country;
10 Farmer in time of frost the burning leagues,
By red-eyed orchards sow the seeds of snow,
In your young years the vegetable century.

And father all nor fail the fly-lord's acre,
Nor sprout on owl-seed like a goblin-sucker,
15 But rail with your wizard's ribs the heart-shaped planet;
Of mortal voices to the ninnies' choir,
High lord esquire, speak up the singing cloud,
And pluck a mandrake music from the marrowroot.

Roll unmanly over this turning tuft,
20 O ring of seas, nor sorrow as I shift
From all my mortal lovers with a starboard smile;
Nor when my love lies in the cross-boned drift
Naked among the bow-and-arrow birds
Shall you turn cockwise on a tufted axle.

25 Who gave these seas their colour in a shape
Shaped my clayfellow, and the heaven's ark
In time at flood filled with his coloured doubles;

O who is glory in the shapeless maps,
Now make the world of me as I have made
30   A merry manshape of your walking circle.

22 *Where once the waters of your face*

Where once the waters of your face
Spun to my screws, your dry ghost blows,
The dead turns up its eye;
Where once the mermen through your ice
5   Pushed up their hair, the dry wind steers
Through salt and root and roe.

Where once your green knots sank their splice
Into the tided cord, there goes
The green unraveller,
10   His scissors oiled, his knife hung loose
To cut the channels at their source
And lay the wet fruits low.

Invisible, your clocking tides
Break on the lovebeds of the weeds;
15   The weed of love's left dry;
There round about your stones the shades
Of children go who, from their voids,
Cry to the dolphined sea.

Dry as a tomb, your coloured lids
20   Shall not be latched while magic glides
Sage on the earth and sky;
There shall be corals in your beds,
There shall be serpents in your tides,
Till all our sea-faiths die.

23   *Our eunuch dreams*

I

Our eunuch dreams, all seedless in the light,
Of light and love, the tempers of the heart,
Whack their boys' limbs,
And, winding-footed in their shawl and sheet,
Groom the dark brides, the widows of the night
Fold in their arms.

The shades of girls, all flavoured from their shrouds,
When sunlight goes are sundered from the worm,
The bones of men, the broken in their beds,
By midnight pulleys that unhouse the tomb.

II

In this our age the gunman and his moll,
Two one-dimensioned ghosts, love on a reel,
Strange to our solid eye,
And speak their midnight nothings as they swell;
When cameras shut they hurry to their hole
Down in the yard of day.

They dance between their arclamps and our skull,
Impose their shots, throwing the nights away;
We watch the show of shadows kiss or kill,
Flavoured of celluloid give love the lie.

III

Which is the world? Of our two sleepings, which
Shall fall awake when cures and their itch
Raise up this red-eyed earth?
Pack off the shapes of daylight and their starch,
The sunny gentlemen, the Welshing rich,
Or drive the night-geared forth.

The photograph is married to the eye,
Grafts on its bride one-sided skins of truth;
The dream has sucked the sleeper of his faith
30   That shrouded men might marrow as they fly.

IV

This is the world: the lying likeness of
Our strips of stuff that tatter as we move
Loving and being loth;
The dream that kicks the buried from their sack
35   And lets their trash be honoured as the quick.
This is the world. Have faith.

For we shall be a shouter like the cock,
Blowing the old dead back; our shots shall smack
The image from the plates;
40   And we shall be fit fellows for a life,
And who remain shall flower as they love,
Praise to our faring hearts.

24 *I see the boys of summer*

I

I see the boys of summer in their ruin
Lay the gold tithings barren,
Setting no store by harvest, freeze the soils;
There in their heat the winter floods
5   Of frozen loves they fetch their girls,
And drown the cargoed apples in their tides.

These boys of light are curdlers in their folly,
Sour the boiling honey;
The jacks of frost they finger in the hives;

10   There in the sun the frigid threads
      Of doubt and dark they feed their nerves;
      The signal moon is zero in their voids.

      I see the summer children in their mothers
      Split up the brawned womb's weathers,
15   Divide the night and day with fairy thumbs;
      There in the deep with quartered shades
      Of sun and moon they paint their dams
      As sunlight paints the shelling of their heads.

      I see that from these boys shall men of nothing
20   Stature by seeding shifting,
      Or lame the air with leaping from its heats;
      There from their hearts the dogdayed pulse
      Of love and light bursts in their throats.
      O see the pulse of summer in the ice.

                        II

25   But seasons must be challenged or they totter
      Into a chiming quarter
      Where, punctual as death, we ring the stars;
      There, in his night, the black-tongued bells
      The sleepy man of winter pulls,
30   Nor blows back moon-and-midnight as she blows.

      We are the dark deniers, let us summon
      Death from a summer woman,
      A muscling life from lovers in their cramp,
      From the fair dead who flush the sea
35   The bright-eyed worm on Davy's lamp,
      And from the planted womb the man of straw.

      We summer boys in this four-winded spinning,
      Green of the seaweeds' iron,
      Hold up the noisy sea and drop her birds,

40   Pick the world's ball of wave and froth
To choke the deserts with her tides,
And comb the county gardens for a wreath.

In spring we cross our foreheads with the holly,
Heigh ho the blood and berry,
45   And nail the merry squires to the trees;
Here love's damp muscle dries and dies,
Here break a kiss in no love's quarry.
O see the poles of promise in the boys.

III

I see you boys of summer in your ruin.
50   Man in his maggot's barren.
And boys are full and foreign in the pouch.
I am the man your father was.
We are the sons of flint and pitch.
O see the poles are kissing as they cross.

25 If I were tickled by the rub of love

If I were tickled by the rub of love,
A rooking girl who stole me for her side,
Broke through her straws, breaking my bandaged string,
If the red tickle as the cattle calve
5   Still set to scratch a laughter from my lung,
I would not fear the apple nor the flood
Nor the bad blood of spring.

Shall it be male or female? say the cells,
And drop the plum like fire from the flesh.
10   If I were tickled by the hatching hair,
The winging bone that sprouted in the heels,

The itch of man upon the baby's thigh,
I would not fear the gallows nor the axe
Nor the crossed sticks of war.

15 Shall it be male or female? say the fingers
That chalk the walls with green girls and their men.
I would not fear the muscling-in of love
If I were tickled by the urchin hungers
Rehearsing heat upon a raw-edged nerve.
20 I would not fear the devil in the loin
Nor the outspoken grave.

If I were tickled by the lovers' rub
That wipes away not crow's-foot nor the lock
Of sick old manhood on the fallen jaws,
25 Time and the crabs and the sweethearting crib
Would leave me cold as butter for the flies,
The sea of scums could drown me as it broke
Dead on the sweethearts' toes.

This world is half the devil's and my own,
30 Daft with the drug that's smoking in a girl
And curling round the bud that forks her eye.
An old man's shank one-marrowed with my bone,
And all the herrings smelling in the sea,
I sit and watch the worm beneath my nail
35 Wearing the quick away.

And that's the rub, the only rub that tickles.
The knobbly ape that swings along his sex
From damp love-darkness and the nurse's twist
Can never raise the midnight of a chuckle,
40 Nor when he finds a beauty in the breast
Of lover, mother, lovers, or his six
Feet in the rubbing dust.

And what's the rub? Death's feather on the nerve?
Your mouth, my love, the thistle in the kiss?
45 My Jack of Christ born thorny on the tree?
The words of death are dryer than his stiff,
My wordy wounds are printed with your hair.
I would be tickled by the rub that is:
Man be my metaphor.

26 *Especially when the October wind*

Especially when the October wind
With frosty fingers punishes my hair,
Caught by the crabbing sun I walk on fire
And cast a shadow crab upon the land,
5 By the sea's side, hearing the noise of birds,
Hearing the raven cough in winter sticks,
My busy heart who shudders as she talks
Sheds the syllabic blood and drains her words.

Shut, too, in a tower of words, I mark
10 On the horizon walking like the trees
The wordy shapes of women, and the rows
Of the star-gestured children in the park.
Some let me make you of the vowelled beeches,
Some of the oaken voices, from the roots
15 Of many a thorny shire tell you notes,
Some let me make you of the water's speeches.

Behind a pot of ferns the wagging clock
Tells me the hour's word, the neural meaning
Flies on the shafted disc, declaims the morning
20 And tells the windy weather in the cock.

Some let me make you of the meadow's signs;
The signal grass that tells me all I know
Breaks with the wormy winter through the eye.
Some let me tell you of the raven's sins.

25   Especially when the October wind
(Some let me make you of autumnal spells,
The spider-tongued, and the loud hill of Wales)
With fist of turnips punishes the land,
Some let me make you of the heartless words.
30   The heart is drained that, spelling in the scurry
Of chemic blood, warned of the coming fury.
By the sea's side hear the dark-vowelled birds.

27 Should lanterns shine

Should lanterns shine, the holy face,
Caught in an octagon of unaccustomed light,
Would wither up, and any boy of love
Look twice before he fell from grace.
5   The features in their private dark
Are formed of flesh, but let the false day come
And from her lips the faded pigments fall,
The mummy cloths expose an ancient breast.

I have been told to reason by the heart,
20   But heart, like head, leads helplessly;
I have been told to reason by the pulse,
And, when it quickens, alter the actions' pace
Till field and roof lie level and the same
So fast I move defying time, the quiet gentleman
15   Whose beard wags in Egyptian wind.

I have heard many years of telling,
And many years should see some change.

The ball I threw while playing in the park
Has not yet reached the ground.

28 from *Altarwise by owl-light*

I

Altarwise by owl-light in the halfway-house
The gentleman lay graveward with his furies;
Abaddon in the hang-nail cracked from Adam,
And, from his fork, a dog among the fairies,
5   The atlas-eater with a jaw for news,
Bit out the mandrake with tomorrow's scream.
Then, penny-eyed, that gentleman of wounds,
Old cock from nowheres and the heaven's egg,
With bones unbuttoned to the halfway winds,
10 Hatched from the windy salvage on one leg,
Scraped at my cradle in a walking word
That night of time under the Christward shelter,
I am the long world's gentleman, he said,
And share my bed with Capricorn and Cancer.

II

Death is all metaphors, shape in one history;
The child that sucketh long is shooting up,
The planet-ducted pelican of circles
Weans on an artery the gender's strip;
5   Child of the short spark in a shapeless country
Soon sets alight a long stick from the cradle;
The horizontal cross-bones of Abaddon,
You by the cavern over the black stairs,

Rung bone and blade, the verticals of Adam,
10   And, manned by midnight, Jacob to the stars;
Hairs of your head, then said the hollow agent,
Are but the roots of nettles and of feathers
Over these groundworks thrusting through a pavement
And hemlock-headed in the wood of weathers.

III

First there was the lamb on knocking knees
And three dead seasons on a climbing grave
That Adam's wether in the flock of horns,
Butt of the tree-tailed worm that mounted Eve,
5   Horned down with skullfoot and the skull of toes
On thunderous pavements in the garden time;
Rip of the vaults, I took my marrow-ladle
Out of the wrinkled undertaker's van,
And, Rip Van Winkle from a timeless cradle,
10   Dipped me breast-deep in the descended bone;
The black ram, shuffling of the year, old winter,
Alone alive among his mutton fold,
We rung our weathering changes on the ladder,
Said the antipodes, and twice spring chimed.

IV

What is the metre of the dictionary?
The size of genesis? the short spark's gender?
Shade without shape? the shape of Pharaoh's echo?
(My shape of age nagging the wounded whisper).
5   Which sixth of wind blew out the burning gentry?
(Questions are hunchbacks to the poker marrow).
What of a bamboo man among your acres?
Corset the boneyards for a crooked lad?
Button your bodice on a hump of splinters,
10   My camel's eye will needle through the shroud.
Love's a reflection of the mushroom features,

Stills snapped by night in the bread-sided field,
Once close-up smiling in the wall of pictures,
Ark-lamped thrown back upon the cutting flood.

V

And from the windy West came two-gunned Gabriel,
From Jesu's sleeve trumped up the king of spots,
The sheath-decked jacks, queen with a shuffled heart;
Said the fake gentleman in suit of spades,
5   Black-tongued and tipsy from salvation's bottle,
Rose my Byzantine Adam in the night;
For loss of blood I fell on Ishmael's plain,
Under the milky mushrooms slew my hunger,
A climbing sea from Asia had me down
10   And Jonah's Moby snatched me by the hair;
Cross-stroked salt Adam to the frozen angel
Pin-legged on pole-hills with a black medusa
By waste seas where the white bear quoted Virgil
And sirens singing from our lady's sea-straw.

29   *The seed-at-zero*

The seed-at-zero shall not storm
That town of ghosts, the trodden womb
With her rampart to his tapping,
No god-in-hero tumble down
5   Like a tower on the town
Dumbly and divinely stumbling
Over the manwaging line.

The seed-at-zero shall not storm
That town of ghosts, the manwaged womb
10   With her rampart to his tapping,
No god-in-hero tumble down

Like a tower on the town
Dumbly and divinely leaping
Over the warbearing line.

15 Through the rampart of the sky
Shall the star-flanked seed be riddled,
Manna for the rumbling ground,
Quickening for the riddled sea;
Settled on a virgin stronghold
20 He shall grapple with the guard
And the keeper of the key.

Through the rampart of the sky
Shall the star-flanked seed be riddled,
Manna for the guarded ground,
25 Quickening for the virgin sea;
Settling on a riddled stronghold
He shall grapple with the guard
And the loser of the key.

May a humble village labour
30 And a continent deny?
A hemisphere may scold him
And a green inch be his bearer;
Let the hero seed find harbour,
Seaports by a drunken shore
35 Have their thirsty sailors hide him.

May a humble planet labour
And a continent deny?
A village green may scold him
And a high sphere be his bearer;
40 Let the hero seed find harbour,
Seaports by a thirsty shore
Have their drunken sailors hide him.

Man-in-seed, in seed-at-zero,
From the foreign fields of space,
45   Shall not thunder on the town
With a star-flanked garrison,
Nor the cannons of his kingdom
Shall the hero-in-tomorrow
Range on the sky-scraping place.

50   Man-in-seed, in seed-at-zero,
From the star-flanked fields of space,
Thunders on the foreign town
With a sand-bagged garrison,
Nor the cannons of his kingdom
55   Shall the hero-in-tomorrow
Range from the grave-groping place.

30 *Then was my neophyte*

Then was my neophyte,
Child in white blood bent on its knees
Under the bell of rocks,
Ducked in the twelve, disciple seas
5   The winder of the water-clocks
Calls a green day and night.
My sea hermaphrodite,
Snail of man in His ship of fires
That burn the bitten decks,
10   Knew all His horrible desires
The climber of the water sex
Calls the green rock of light.

Who in these labyrinths,
This tidethread and the lane of scales,
15   Twine in a moon-blown shell,

Escapes to the flat cities' sails
Furled on the fishes' house and hell,
Nor falls to His green myths?
Stretch the salt photographs,
20   The landscape grief, love in His oils
Mirror from man to whale
That the green child see like a grail
Through veil and fin and fire and coil
Time on the canvas paths.

25   He films my vanity.
Shot in the wind, by tilted arcs,
Over the water come
Children from homes and children's parks
Who speak on a finger and thumb,
30   And the masked, headless boy.
His reels and mystery
The winder of the clockwise scene
Wound like a ball of lakes
Then threw on that tide-hoisted screen
35   Love's image till my heartbone breaks
By a dramatic sea.

Who kills my history?
The year-hedged row is lame with flint,
Blunt scythe and water blade.
40   'Who could snap off the shapeless print
From your tomorrow-treading shade
With oracle for eye?'
Time kills me terribly.
'Time shall not murder you,' He said,
45   'Nor the green nought be hurt;
Who could hack out your unsucked heart,
O green and unborn and undead?'
I saw time murder me.

31   It is the sinners' dust-tongued bell

It is the sinners' dust-tongued bell claps me to churches
When, with his torch and hourglass, like a sulphur priest,
His beast heel cleft in a sandal,
Time marks a black aisle kindle from the brand of ashes,
Grief with dishevelled hands tear out the altar ghost
And a firewind kill the candle.

Over the choir minute I hear the hour chant:
Time's coral saint and the salt grief drown a foul sepulchre
And a whirlpool drives the prayerwheel;
Moonfall and sailing emperor, pale as their tideprint,
Hear by death's accident the clocked and dashed-down spire
Strike the sea hour through bellmetal.

There is loud and dark directly under the dumb flame,
Storm, snow, and fountain in the weather of fireworks,
Cathedral calm in the pulled house;
Grief with drenched book and candle christens the cherub time
From the emerald, still bell; and from the pacing weathercock
The voice of bird on coral prays.

Forever it is a white child in the dark-skinned summer
Out of the font of bone and plants at that stone tocsin
Scales the blue wall of spirits;
From blank and leaking winter sails the child in colour,
Shakes, in crabbed burial shawl, by sorcerer's insect woken,
Ding dong from the mute turrets.

I mean by time the cast and curfew rascal of our marriage,
At nightbreak born in the fat side, from an animal bed
In a holy room in a wave;

And all love's sinners in sweet cloth kneel to a hyleg image,
Nutmeg, civet, and sea-parsley serve the plagued groom and
    bride
30 Who have brought forth the urchin grief.

32 *How shall my animal*

How shall my animal
Whose wizard shape I trace in the cavernous skull,
Vessel of abscesses and exultation's shell,
Endure burial under the spelling wall,
5 The invoked, shrouding veil at the cap of the face,
Who should be furious,
Drunk as a vineyard snail, flailed like an octopus,
Roaring, crawling, quarrel
With the outside weathers,
10 The natural circle of the discovered skies
Draw down to its weird eyes?

How shall it magnetize,
Towards the studded male in a bent, midnight blaze
That melts the lionhead's heel and horseshoe of the heart,
15 A brute land in the cool top of the country days
To trot with a loud mate the haybeds of a mile,
Love and labour and kill
In quick, sweet, cruel light till the locked ground sprout out,
The black, burst sea rejoice,
20 The bowels turn turtle,
Claw of the crabbed veins squeeze from each red particle
The parched and raging voice?

Fishermen of mermen
Creep and harp on the tide, sinking their charmed, bent pin
25 With bridebait of gold bread, I with a living skein,

Tongue and ear in the thread, angle the temple-bound
Curl-locked and animal cavepools of spells and bone,
Trace out a tentacle,
Nailed with an open eye, in the bowl of wounds and weed
30   To clasp my fury on ground
And clap its great blood down;
Never shall beast be born to atlas the few seas
Or poise the day on a horn.

Sigh long, clay cold, lie shorn,
35   Cast high, stunned on gilled stone; sly scissors ground in frost
Clack through the thicket of strength, love hewn in pillars drops
With carved bird, saint, and sun, the wrackspiked maiden mouth
Lops, as a bush plumed with flames, the rant of the fierce eye,
Clips short the gesture of breath.
40   Die in red feathers when the flying heaven's cut,
And roll with the knocked earth:
Lie dry, rest robbed, my beast.
You have kicked from a dark den, leaped up the whinnying
         light,
And dug your grave in my breast.

33   After the funeral
   (In memory of Ann Jones)

After the funeral, mule praises, brays,
Windshake of sailshaped ears, muffle-toed tap
Tap happily of one peg in the thick
Grave's foot, blinds down the lids, the teeth in black,
5   The spittled eyes, the salt ponds in the sleeves,
Morning smack of the spade that wakes up sleep,
Shakes a desolate boy who slits his throat
In the dark of the coffin and sheds dry leaves,
That breaks one bone to light with a judgment clout,

10   After the feast of tear-stuffed time and thistles
In a room with a stuffed fox and a stale fern,
I stand, for this memorial's sake, alone
In the snivelling hours with dead, humped Ann
Whose hooded, fountain heart once fell in puddles
15   Round the parched worlds of Wales and drowned each sun
(Though this for her is a monstrous image blindly
Magnified out of praise; her death was a still drop;
She would not have me sinking in the holy
Flood of her heart's fame; she would lie dumb and deep
20   And need no druid of her broken body).
But I, Ann's bard on a raised hearth, call all
The seas to service that her wood-tongued virtue
Babble like a bellbuoy over the hymning heads,
Bow down the walls of the ferned and foxy woods
25   That her love sing and swing through a brown chapel,
Bless her bent spirit with four, crossing birds.
Her flesh was meek as milk, but this skyward statue
With the wild breast and blessed and giant skull
Is carved from her in a room with a wet window
30   In a fiercely mourning house in a crooked year.
I know her scrubbed and sour humble hands
Lie with religion in their cramp, her threadbare
Whisper in a damp word, her wits drilled hollow,
Her fist of a face died clenched on a round pain;
35   And sculptured Ann is seventy years of stone.
These cloud-sopped, marble hands, this monumental
Argument of the hewn voice, gesture and psalm
Storm me forever over her grave until
The stuffed lung of the fox twitch and cry Love
40   And the strutting fern lay seeds on the black sill.

34 *The tombstone told*

The tombstone told when she died.
Her two surnames stopped me still.
A virgin married at rest.
She married in this pouring place,
5   That I struck one day by luck,
Before I heard in my mother's side
Or saw in the looking-glass shell
The rain through her cold heart speak
And the sun killed in her face.
10   More the thick stone cannot tell.

Before she lay on a stranger's bed
With a hand plunged through her hair,
Or that rainy tongue beat back
Through the devilish years and innocent deaths
15   To the room of a secret child,
Among men later I heard it said
She cried her white-dressed limbs were bare
And her red lips were kissed black,
She wept in her pain and made mouths,
20   Talked and tore though her eyes smiled.

I who saw in a hurried film
Death and this mad heroine
Meet once on a mortal wall
Heard her speak through the chipped beak
25   Of the stone bird guarding her:
I died before bedtime came
But my womb was bellowing
And I felt with my bare fall
A blazing red harsh head tear up
30   And the dear floods of his hair.

35   On no work of words

On no work of words now for three lean months in the bloody
Belly of the rich year and the big purse of my body
I bitterly take to task my poverty and craft:

To take to give is all, return what is hungrily given
5   Puffing the pounds of manna up through the dew to heaven,
The lovely gift of the gab bangs back on a blind shaft.

To lift to leave from the treasures of man is pleasing death
That will rake at last all currencies of the marked breath
And count the taken, forsaken mysteries in a bad dark.

10   To surrender now is to pay the expensive ogre twice.
Ancient woods of my blood, dash down to the nut of the seas
If I take to burn or return this world which is each man's work.

36   Twenty-four years

Twenty-four years remind the tears of my eyes.
(Bury the dead for fear that they walk to the grave in labour.)
In the groin of the natural doorway I crouched like a tailor
Sewing a shroud for a journey
5   By the light of the meat-eating sun.
Dressed to die, the sensual strut begun,
With my red veins full of money,
In the final direction of the elementary town
I advance for as long as forever is.

37 Once it was the colour of saying

Once it was the colour of saying
Soaked my table the uglier side of a hill
With a capsized field where a school sat still
And a black and white patch of girls grew playing;
The gentle seaslides of saying I must undo
That all the charmingly drowned arise to cockcrow and kill.
When I whistled with mitching boys through a reservoir park
Where at night we stoned the cold and cuckoo
Lovers in the dirt of their leafy beds,
The shade of their trees was a word of many shades
And a lamp of lightning for the poor in the dark;
Now my saying shall be my undoing,
And every stone I wind off like a reel.

38 Because the pleasure-bird whistles

Because the pleasure-bird whistles after the hot wires,
Shall the blind horse sing sweeter?
Convenient bird and beast lie lodged to suffer
The supper and knives of a mood.
In the sniffed and poured snow on the tip of the tongue of the
     year
That clouts the spittle like bubbles with broken rooms,
An enamoured man alone by the twigs of his eyes, two fires,
Camped in the drug-white shower of nerves and food,
Savours the lick of the times through a deadly wood of hair
In a wind that plucked a goose,
Nor ever, as the wild tongue breaks its tombs,
Rounds to look at the red, wagged root.
Because there stands, one story out of the bum city,
That frozen wife whose juices drift like a fixed sea

15   Secretly in statuary,
      Shall I, struck on the hot and rocking street,
      Not spin to stare at an old year
      Toppling and burning in the muddle of towers and galleries
      Like the mauled pictures of boys?
20   The salt person and blasted place
      I furnish with the meat of a fable;
      If the dead starve, their stomachs turn to tumble
      An upright man in the antipodes
      Or spray-based and rock-chested sea:
25   Over the past table I repeat this present grace.

39 *If my head hurt a hair's foot*

      'If my head hurt a hair's foot
      Pack back the downed bone. If the unpricked ball of my breath
      Bump on a spout let the bubbles jump out.
      Sooner drop with the worm of the ropes round my throat
5   Than bully ill love in the clouted scene.

      All game phrases fit your ring of a cockfight:
      I'll comb the snared woods with a glove on a lamp,
      Peck, sprint, dance on fountains and duck time
      Before I rush in a crouch the ghost with a hammer, air,
10   Strike light, and bloody a loud room.

      If my bunched, monkey coming is cruel
      Rage me back to the making house. My hand unravel
      When you sew the deep door. The bed is a cross place.
      Bend, if my journey ache, direction like an arc or make
15   A limp and riderless shape to leap nine thinning months.'

'No. Not for Christ's dazzling bed
Or a nacreous sleep among soft particles and charms
My dear would I change my tears or your iron head.
Thrust, my daughter or son, to escape, there is none, none,
    none,
20   Nor when all ponderous heaven's host of waters breaks.

Now to awake hushed of gestures and my joy like a cave
To the anguish and carrion, to the infant forever unfree,
O my lost love bounced from a good home;
The grain that hurries this way from the rim of the grave
25   Has a voice and a house, and there and here you must couch
    and cry.

Rest beyond choice in the dust-appointed grain,
At the breast stored with seas. No return
Through the waves of the fat streets nor the skeleton's thin
    ways.
The grave and my calm body are shut to your coming as stone,
30   And the endless beginning of prodigies suffers open.'

40   *To Others than You*

Friend by enemy I call you out.

You with a bad coin in your socket,
You my friend there with a winning air
Who palmed the lie on me when you looked
5   Brassily at my shyest secret,
Enticed with twinkling bits of the eye
Till the sweet tooth of my love bit dry,
Rasped at last, and I stumbled and sucked,
Whom now I conjure to stand as thief
10   In the memory worked by mirrors,

With unforgettably smiling act,
Quickness of hand in the velvet glove
And my whole heart under your hammer,
Were once such a creature, so gay and frank
15 A desireless familiar
I never thought to utter or think
While you displaced a truth in the air,

That though I loved them for their faults
As much as for their good,
20 My friends were enemies on stilts
With their heads in a cunning cloud.

41 *When I woke*

When I woke, the town spoke.
Birds and clocks and cross bells
Dinned aside the coiling crowd,
The reptile profligates in a flame,
5 Spoilers and pokers of sleep,
The next-door sea dispelled
Frogs and satans and woman-luck,
While a man outside with a billhook,
Up to his head in his blood,
10 Cutting the morning off,
The warm-veined double of Time
And his scarving beard from a book,
Slashed down the last snake as though
It were a wand or subtle bough,
15 Its tongue peeled in the wrap of a leaf.

Every morning I make,
God in bed, good and bad,
After a water-face walk,

The death-staggered scatter-breath
20   Mammoth and sparrowfall
Everybody's earth.
Where birds ride like leaves and boats like ducks
I heard, this morning, waking,
Crossly out of the town noises
25   A voice in the erected air,
No prophet-progeny of mine,
Cry my sea town was breaking.
No Time, spoke the clocks, no God, rang the bells,
I drew the white sheet over the islands
30   And the coins on my eyelids sang like shells.

42 *Paper and sticks*

Paper and sticks and shovel and match
Why won't the news of the old world catch
And the fire in a temper start

Once I had a rich boy for myself
5   I loved his body and his navy blue wealth
And I lived in his purse and his heart

When in our bed I was tossing and turning
All I could see were his brown eyes burning
By the green of a one pound note

10   I talk to him as I clean the grate
O my dear it's never too late
To take me away as you whispered and wrote

I had a handsome and well-off boy
I'll share my money and we'll run for joy
15   With a bouncing and silver spooned kid

Sharp and shrill my silly tongue scratches
Words on the air as the fire catches
You never did and *he* never did.

43   *Once below a time*

I

Once below a time,
When my pinned-around-the-spirit
Cut-to-measure flesh bit,
Suit for a serial sum
5   On the first of each hardship,
My paid-for slaved-for own too late
In love torn breeches and blistered jacket
On the snapping rims of the ashpit,
In grottoes I worked with birds,
10   Spiked with mastiff collar,
Tasselled in cellar and snipping shop
Or decked on a cloud swallower,

Then swift from a bursting sea with bottlecork boats
And out-of-perspective sailors,
15   In common clay clothes disguised as scales,
As a he-god's paddling water skirts,
I astounded the sitting tailors,
I set back the clock faced tailors,

Then, bushily swanked in bear wig and tails,
20   Hopping hot leaved and feathered
From the kangaroo foot of the earth,
From the chill, silent centre
Trailing the frost bitten cloth,
Up through the lubber crust of Wales
25   I rocketed to astonish

The flashing needle rock of squatters,
The criers of Shabby and Shorten,
The famous stitch droppers.

II

My silly suit, hardly yet suffered for,
30   Around some coffin carrying
Birdman or told ghost I hung.
And the owl hood, the heel hider,
Claw fold and hole for the rotten
Head, deceived, I believed, my maker,

35   The cloud perched tailors' master with nerves for cotton.
On the old seas from stories, thrashing my wings,
Combing with antlers, Columbus on fire,
I was pierced by the idol tailor's eyes,
Glared through shark mask and navigating head,
40   Cold Nansen's beak on a boat full of gongs,

To the boy of common thread,
The bright pretender, the ridiculous sea dandy
With dry flesh and earth for adorning and bed.
It was sweet to drown in the readymade handy water
45   With my cherry capped dangler green as seaweed
Summoning a child's voice from a webfoot stone,
Never never oh never to regret the bugle I wore
On my cleaving arm as I blasted in a wave.

Now shown and mostly bare I would lie down,
50   Lie down, lie down and live
As quiet as a bone.

44 There was a saviour

There was a saviour
Rarer than radium,
Commoner than water, crueller than truth;
Children kept from the sun
Assembled at his tongue
To hear the golden note turn in a groove,
Prisoners of wishes locked their eyes
In the jails and studies of his keyless smiles.

The voice of children says
From a lost wilderness
There was calm to be done in his safe unrest,
When hindering man hurt
Man, animal, or bird
We hid our fears in that murdering breath,
Silence, silence to do, when earth grew loud,
In lairs and asylums of the tremendous shout.

There was glory to hear
In the churches of his tears,
Under his downy arm you sighed as he struck,
O you who could not cry
On to the ground when a man died
Put a tear for joy in the unearthly flood
And laid your cheek against a cloud-formed shell:
Now in the dark there is only yourself and myself.

Two proud, blacked brothers cry,
Winter-locked side by side,
To this inhospitable hollow year,
O we who could not stir
One lean sigh when we heard

30   Greed on man beating near and fire neighbour
But wailed and nested in the sky-blue wall
Now break a giant tear for the little known fall,

For the drooping of homes
That did not nurse our bones,
35   Brave deaths of only ones but never found,
Now see, alone in us,
Our own true strangers' dust
Ride through the doors of our unentered house.
Exiled in us we arouse the soft,
40   Unclenched, armless, silk and rough love that breaks all rocks.

45   *Into her lying down head*

I

Into her lying down head
His enemies entered bed,
Under the encumbered eyelid,
Through the rippled drum of the hair-buried ear;
5   And Noah's rekindled now unkind dove
Flew man-bearing there.
Last night in a raping wave
Whales unreined from the green grave
In fountains of origin gave up their love,
10   Along her innocence glided
Juan aflame and savagely young King Lear,
Queen Catherine howling bare
And Samson drowned in his hair,
The colossal intimacies of silent
15   Once seen strangers or shades on a stair;
There the dark blade and wanton sighing her down

To a haycock couch and the scythes of his arms
>> Rode and whistled a hundred times
>> Before the crowing morning climbed;
20 Man was the burning England she was sleep-walking, and the
enamouring island
>> Made her limbs by luminous charms,
Sleep to a newborn sleep in a swaddling loin-leaf stroked and
sang
>> And his runaway beloved childlike laid in the acorned
sand.

II

>> There where a numberless tongue
25 >> Wound their room with a male moan,
> His faith around her flew undone
And darkness hung the walls with baskets of snakes,
A furnace-nostrilled column-membered
>> Super-or-near man
30 >> Resembling to her dulled sense
>> The thief of adolescence,
Early imaginary half remembered
>> Oceanic lover alone
Jealously cannot forget for all her sakes,
35 >> Made his bad bed in her good
>> Night, and enjoyed as he would.
Crying, white gowned, from the middle moonlit stages
>> Out to the tiered and hearing tide,
Close and far she announced the theft of the heart
40 In the taken body at many ages,
>> Trespasser and broken bride
>> Celebrating at her side
All blood-signed assailings and vanished marriages in which he
had no lovely part
>> Nor could share, for his pride, to the least

45   Mutter and foul wingbeat of the solemnizing nightpriest
     Her holy unholy hours with the always anonymous beast.

III

Two sand grains together in bed,
Head to heaven-circling head,
Singly lie with the whole wide shore,
50   The covering sea their nightfall with no names;
And out of every domed and soil-based shell
One voice in chains declaims
The female, deadly, and male
Libidinous betrayal,
55   Golden dissolving under the water veil.
A she bird sleeping brittle by
Her lover's wings that fold tomorrow's flight,
Within the nested treefork
Sings to the treading hawk
60   Carrion, paradise, chirrup my bright yolk.
A blade of grass longs with the meadow,
A stone lies lost and locked in the lark-high hill.
Open as to the air to the naked shadow
O she lies alone and still,
65   Innocent between two wars,
With the incestuous secret brother in the seconds to perpetuate
the stars,
A man torn up mourns in the sole night.
And the second comers, the severers, the enemies from the
deep
Forgotten dark, rest their pulse and bury their dead in her
faithless sleep.

46 *The Countryman's Return*

Embracing low-falutin
London (said the odd man in
A country pot, his hutch in
The fields, by a motherlike henrun)
5   With my fishtail hands and gently
Manuring popeye or
Swelling in flea-specked linen
The rankest of the city
I spent my unwasteable
10   Time among walking pintables
With sprung and padded shoulders,
Tomorrow's drunk club majors
Growing their wounds already,
The last war's professional
15   Unclaimed dead, girls from good homes
Studying the testicle
In communal crab flats
With the Sunflowers laid on,
Old paint-stained tumblers riding
20   On stools to a one man show down,
Gasketted and sirensuited
Bored and viciously waiting
Nightingales of the casualty stations
In the afternoon wasters
25   White feathering the living.

London's arches are falling
In, in Pedro's or Wendy's
With a silverfox farmer
Trying his hand at failing
30   Again, a collected poet
And some dismantled women,
Razor man and belly king,

I propped humanity's weight
Against the fruit machine,
35   Opened my breast and into
The spongebag let them all melt.
Zip once more for a traveller
With his goods under his eyes,
Another with hers under her belt,
40   The black man bleached to his tide
Mark, trumpet lipped and blackhead
Eyed, while the tears drag on the tail,
The weighing-scales, of my hand.
Then into blind streets I swam
45   Alone with my bouncing bag,
Too full to bow to the dim
Moon with a relation's face
Or lift my hat to unseen
Brothers dodging through the fog
50   The affectionate pickpocket
And childish, snivelling queen.

Beggars, robbers, inveiglers,
Voices from manholes and drains,
Maternal short time pieces,
55   Octopuses in doorways,
Dark inviters to keyholes
And evenings with great danes,
Bedsitting girls on the beat
With nothing for the metre,
60   Others whose single beds hold two
Only to make two ends meet,
All the hypnotised city's
Insidious procession
Hawking for money and pity
65   Among the hardly possessed.
And I in the wanting sway
Caught among never enough

Conjured me to resemble
A singing Walt from the mower
70 And jerrystone trim villas
Of the upper of the lower half,
Beardlessly wagging in Dean Street,
Blessing and counting the bustling
Twolegged handbagged sparrows,
75 Flogging into the porches
My cavernous, featherbed self.

Cut. Cut the crushed streets, leaving
A hole of errands and shades;
Plug the paper-blowing tubes;
80 Emasculate the seedy clocks;
Rub off the scrawl of prints on
Body and air and building;
Branch and leaf the birdless roofs;
Faces of melting visions,
85 Magdalene prostitution,
Glamour of the bloodily bowed,
Exaltation of the blind,
That sin-embracing dripper of fun
Sweep away like a cream cloud;
90 Bury all rubbish and love signs
Of my week in the dirtbox
In this anachronistic scene
Where sitting in clean linen
In a hutch in a cowpatched glen
95 Now I delight, I suppose, in
The countryman's return
And count by birds' eggs and leaves
The rusticating minutes,
The wasteful hushes among trees.
100 And O to cut the green field, leaving
One rich street with hunger in it.

47 *Deaths and Entrances*

On almost the incendiary eve
    Of several near deaths,
When one at the great least of your best loved
    And always known must leave
Lions and fires of his flying breath,
    Of your immortal friends
Who'd raise the organs of the counted dust
    To shoot and sing your praise,
One who called deepest down shall hold his peace
    That cannot sink or cease
    Endlessly to his wound
In many married London's estranging grief.

On almost the incendiary eve
    When at your lips and keys,
Locking, unlocking, the murdered strangers weave,
    One who is most unknown,
Your polestar neighbour, sun of another street,
    Will dive up to his tears.
He'll bathe his raining blood in the male sea
    Who strode for your own dead
And wind his globe out of your water thread
    And load the throats of shells
    With every cry since light
Flashed first across his thunderclapping eyes.

On almost the incendiary eve
    Of deaths and entrances,
When near and strange wounded on London's waves
    Have sought your single grave,
One enemy, of many, who knows well
    Your heart is luminous

In the watched dark, quivering through locks and caves,
   Will pull the thunderbolts
To shut the sun, plunge, mount your darkened keys
   And sear just riders back,
35   Until that one loved least
Looms the last Samson of your zodiac.

48 *Ballad of the Long-legged Bait*

The bows glided down, and the coast
Blackened with birds took a last look
At his thrashing hair and whale-blue eye;
The trodden town rang its cobbles for luck.

5 Then goodbye to the fishermanned
Boat with its anchor free and fast
As a bird hooking over the sea,
High and dry by the top of the mast,

Whispered the affectionate sand
10 And the bulwarks of the dazzled quay.
For my sake sail, and never look back,
Said the looking land.

Sails drank the wind, and white as milk
He sped into the drinking dark;
15 The sun shipwrecked west on a pearl
And the moon swam out of its hulk.

Funnels and masts went by in a whirl.
Goodbye to the man on the sea-legged deck
To the gold gut that sings on his reel
20 To the bait that stalked out of the sack,

For we saw him throw to the swift flood
A girl alive with his hooks through her lips;
All the fishes were rayed in blood,
Said the dwindling ships.

25 Goodbye to chimneys and funnels,
Old wives that spin in the smoke,
He was blind to the eyes of candles
In the praying windows of waves

But heard his bait buck in the wake
30 And tussle in a shoal of loves.
Now cast down your rod, for the whole
Of the sea is hilly with whales,

She longs among horses and angels,
The rainbow-fish bend in her joys,
35 Floated the lost cathedral
Chimes of the rocked buoys.

Where the anchor rode like a gull
Miles over the moonstruck boat
A squall of birds bellowed and fell,
40 A cloud blew the rain from its throat;

He saw the storm smoke to kill
With fuming bows and ram of ice,
Fire on starlight, rake Jesu's stream;
And nothing shone on the water's face

45 But the oil and bubble of the moon,
Plunging and piercing in his course
The lured fish under the foam
Witnessed with a kiss.

Whales in the wake like capes and Alps
50   Quaked the sick sea and snouted deep,
Deep the great bushed bait with raining lips
Slipped the fins of those humpbacked tons

And fled their love in a weaving dip.
Oh, Jericho was falling in their lungs!
55   She nipped and dived in the nick of love,
Spun on a spout like a long-legged ball

Till every beast blared down in a swerve
Till every turtle crushed from his shell
Till every bone in the rushing grave
60   Rose and crowed and fell!

Good luck to the hand on the rod,
There is thunder under its thumbs;
Gold gut is a lightning thread,
His fiery reel sings off its flames,

65   The whirled boat in the burn of his blood
Is crying from nets to knives,
Oh the shearwater birds and their boatsized brood
Oh the bulls of Biscay and their calves

Are making under the green, laid veil
70   The long-legged beautiful bait their wives.
Break the black news and paint on a sail
Huge weddings in the waves,

Over the wakeward-flashing spray
Over the gardens of the floor
75   Clash out the mounting dolphin's day,
My mast is a bell-spire,

Strike and smoothe, for my decks are drums,
Sing through the water-spoken prow
The octopus walking into her limbs
80   The polar eagle with his tread of snow.

From salt-lipped beak to the kick of the stern
Sing how the seal has kissed her dead!
The long, laid minute's bride drifts on
Old in her cruel bed.

85   Over the graveyard in the water
Mountains and galleries beneath
Nightingale and hyena
Rejoicing for that drifting death

Sing and howl through sand and anemone
90   Valley and sahara in a shell,
Oh all the wanting flesh his enemy
Thrown to the sea in the shell of a girl

Is old as water and plain as an eel;
Always goodbye to the long-legged bread
95   Scattered in the paths of his heels
For the salty birds fluttered and fed

And the tall grains foamed in their bills;
Always goodbye to the fires of the face,
For the crab-backed dead on the sea-bed rose
100   And scuttled over her eyes,

The blind, clawed stare is cold as sleet.
The tempter under the eyelid
Who shows to the selves asleep
Mast-high moon-white women naked

105   Walking in wishes and lovely for shame
      Is dumb and gone with his flame of brides.
      Susanna's drowned in the bearded stream
      And no-one stirs at Sheba's side

      But the hungry kings of the tides;
110   Sin who had a woman's shape
      Sleeps till Silence blows on a cloud
      And all the lifted waters walk and leap.

      Lucifer that bird's dropping
      Out of the sides of the north
115   Has melted away and is lost
      Is always lost in her vaulted breath,

      Venus lies star-struck in her wound
      And the sensual ruins make
      Seasons over the liquid world,
120   White springs in the dark.

      Always goodbye, cried the voices through the shell,
      Goodbye always for the flesh is cast
      And the fisherman winds his reel
      With no more desire than a ghost.

125   Always good luck, praised the finned in the feather
      Bird after dark and the laughing fish
      As the sails drank up the hail of thunder
      And the long-tailed lightning lit his catch.

      The boat swims into the six-year weather,
130   A wind throws a shadow and it freezes fast.
      See what the gold gut drags from under
      Mountains and galleries to the crest!

See what clings to hair and skull
As the boat skims on with drinking wings!
135   The statues of great rain stand still,
And the flakes fall like hills.

Sing and strike his heavy haul
Toppling up the boatside in a snow of light!
His decks are drenched with miracles.
140   Oh miracle of fishes! The long dead bite!

Out of the urn the size of a man
Out of the room the weight of his trouble
Out of the house that holds a town
In the continent of a fossil

145   One by one in dust and shawl,
Dry as echoes and insect-faced,
His fathers cling to the hand of the girl
And the dead hand leads the past,

Leads them as children and as air
150   On to the blindly tossing tops;
The centuries throw back their hair
And the old men sing from newborn lips:

Time is bearing another son.
Kill Time! She turns in her pain!
155   *The oak is felled in the acorn*
And the hawk in the egg kills the wren.

He who blew the great fire in
And died on a hiss of flames
Or walked on the earth in the evening
160   Counting the denials of the grains

Clings to her drifting hair, and climbs;
And he who taught their lips to sing
Weeps like the risen sun among
The liquid choirs of his tribes.

165 The rod bends low, divining land,
And through the sundered water crawls
A garden holding to her hand
With birds and animals

With men and women and waterfalls
170 Trees cool and dry in the whirlpool of ships
And stunned and still on the green, laid veil
Sand with legends in its virgin laps

And prophets loud on the burned dunes;
Insects and valleys hold her thighs hard,
175 Time and places grip her breast bone,
She is breaking with seasons and clouds;

Round her trailed wrist fresh water weaves,
With moving fish and rounded stones
Up and down the greater waves
180 A separate river breathes and runs;

Strike and sing his catch of fields
For the surge is sown with barley,
The cattle graze on the covered foam,
The hills have footed the waves away,

185 With wild sea fillies and soaking bridles
With salty colts and gales in their limbs
All the horses of his haul of miracles
Gallop through the arched, green farms,

Trot and gallop with gulls upon them
190 And thunderbolts in their manes.
O Rome and Sodom Tomorrow and London
The country tide is cobbled with towns,

And steeples pierce the cloud on her shoulder
And the streets that the fisherman combed
195 When his long-legged flesh was a wind on fire
And his loin was a hunting flame

Coil from the thoroughfares of her hair
And terribly lead him home alive
Lead her prodigal home to his terror,
200 The furious ox-killing house of love.

Down, down, down, under the ground,
Under the floating villages,
Turns the moon-chained and water-wound
Metropolis of fishes,

205 There is nothing left of the sea but its sound,
Under the earth the loud sea walks,
In deathbeds of orchards the boat dies down
And the bait is drowned among hayricks,

Land, land, land, nothing remains
210 Of the pacing, famous sea but its speech,
And into its talkative seven tombs
The anchor dives through the floors of a church.

Goodbye, good luck, struck the sun and the moon,
To the fisherman lost on the land.
215 He stands alone at the door of his home,
With his long-legged heart in his hand.

49   On the Marriage of a Virgin

Waking alone in a multitude of loves when morning's light
Surprised in the opening of her nightlong eyes
His golden yesterday asleep upon the iris
And this day's sun leapt up the sky out of her thighs
5 Was miraculous virginity old as loaves and fishes,
Though the moment of a miracle is unending lightning
And the shipyards of Galilee's footprints hide a navy of doves.

No longer will the vibrations of the sun desire on
Her deepsea pillow where once she married alone,
10 Her heart all ears and eyes, lips catching the avalanche
Of the golden ghost who ringed with his streams her mercury
    bone,
Who under the lids of her windows hoisted his golden luggage,
For a man sleeps where fire leapt down and she learns through
    his arm
That other sun, the jealous coursing of the unrivalled blood.

50   The hunchback in the park

The hunchback in the park
A solitary mister
Propped between trees and water
From the opening of the garden lock
5 That lets the trees and water enter
Until the Sunday sombre bell at dark

Eating bread from a newspaper
Drinking water from the chained cup
That the children filled with gravel

10   In the fountain basin where I sailed my ship
      Slept at night in a dog kennel
      But nobody chained him up.

      Like the park birds he came early
      Like the water he sat down
15   And Mister they called Hey mister
      The truant boys from the town
      Running when he had heard them clearly
      On out of sound

      Past lake and rockery
20   Laughing when he shook his paper
      Hunchbacked in mockery
      Through the loud zoo of the willow groves
      Dodging the park keeper
      With his stick that picked up leaves.

25   And the old dog sleeper
      Alone between nurses and swans
      While the boys among willows
      Made the tigers jump out of their eyes
      To roar on the rockery stones
30   And the groves were blue with sailors

      Made all day until bell time
      A woman figure without fault
      Straight as a young elm
      Straight and tall from his crooked bones
35   That she might stand in the night
      After the locks and chains

      All night in the unmade park
      After the railings and shrubberies
      The birds the grass the trees the lake

40 And the wild boys innocent as strawberries
Had followed the hunchback
To his kennel in the dark.

51 *Among those Killed in the Dawn Raid*
was a Man Aged a Hundred

When the morning was waking over the war
He put on his clothes and stepped out and he died,
The locks yawned loose and a blast blew them wide,
He dropped where he loved on the burst pavement stone
5 And the funeral grains of the slaughtered floor.
Tell his street on its back he stopped a sun
And the craters of his eyes grew springshoots and fire
When all the keys shot from the locks, and rang.
Dig no more for the chains of his grey-haired heart.
10 The heavenly ambulance drawn by a wound
Assembling waits for the spade's ring on the cage.
O keep his bones away from that common cart,
The morning is flying on the wings of his age
And a hundred storks perch on the sun's right hand.

52 *Lie still, sleep becalmed*

Lie still, sleep becalmed, sufferer with the wound
In the throat, burning and turning. All night afloat
On the silent sea we have heard the sound
That came from the wound wrapped in the salt sheet.

5   Under the mile off moon we trembled listening
To the sea sound flowing like blood from the loud wound
And when the salt sheet broke in a storm of singing
The voices of all the drowned swam on the wind.

Open a pathway through the slow sad sail,
10   Throw wide to the wind the gates of the wandering boat
For my voyage to begin to the end of my wound,
We heard the sea sound sing, we saw the salt sheet tell.
Lie still, sleep becalmed, hide the mouth in the throat,
Or we shall obey, and ride with you through the drowned.

53   *Ceremony After a Fire Raid*

I

Myselves
The grievers
Grieve
Among the street burned to tireless death
5   A child of a few hours
With its kneading mouth
Charred on the black breast of the grave
The mother dug, and its arms full of fires.

Begin
10   With singing
Sing
Darkness kindled back into beginning
When the caught tongue nodded blind,
A star was broken
15   Into the centuries of the child
Myselves grieve now, and miracles cannot atone.

Forgive
Us forgive
Give
20   Us your death that myselves the believers
May hold it in a great flood
Till the blood shall spurt,
And the dust shall sing like a bird
As the grains blow, as your death grows, through our heart.

25   Crying
Your dying
Cry,
Child beyond cockcrow, by the fire-dwarfed
Street we chant the flying sea
30   In the body bereft.
Love is the last light spoken. Oh
Seed of sons in the loin of the black husk left.

II

I know not whether
Adam or Eve, the adorned holy bullock
35   Or the white ewe lamb
Or the chosen virgin
Laid in her snow
On the altar of London,
Was the first to die
40   In the cinder of the little skull,
O bride and bride groom
O Adam and Eve together
Lying in the lull
Under the sad breast of the head stone
45   White as the skeleton
Of the garden of Eden.

I know the legend
Of Adam and Eve is never for a second
Silent in my service
50 Over the dead infants
Over the one
Child who was priest and servants,
Word, singers, and tongue
In the cinder of the little skull,
55 Who was the serpent's
Night fall and the fruit like a sun,
Man and woman undone,
Beginning crumbled back to darkness
Bare as the nurseries
60 Of the garden of wilderness.

III

Into the organpipes and steeples
Of the luminous cathedrals,
Into the weathercocks' molten mouths
Rippling in twelve-winded circles,
65 Into the dead clock burning the hour
Over the urn of sabbaths
Over the whirling ditch of daybreak
Over the sun's hovel and the slum of fire
And the golden pavements laid in requiems,
70 Into the cauldrons of the statuary,
Into the bread in a wheatfield of flames,
Into the wine burning like brandy,
The masses of the sea
The masses of the sea under
75 The masses of the infant-bearing sea
Erupt, fountain, and enter to utter for ever
Glory glory glory
The sundering ultimate kingdom of genesis' thunder.

54 Poem in October

It was my thirtieth year to heaven
Woke to my hearing from harbour and neighbour wood
And the mussel pooled and the heron
Priested shore
5   The morning beckon
With water praying and call of seagull and rook
And the knock of sailing boats on the net webbed wall
Myself to set foot
That second
10   In the still sleeping town and set forth.

My birthday began with the water-
Birds and the birds of the winged trees flying my name
Above the farms and the white horses
And I rose
15   In rainy autumn
And walked abroad in a shower of all my days.
High tide and the heron dived when I took the road
Over the border
And the gates
20   Of the town closed as the town awoke.

A springful of larks in a rolling
Cloud and the roadside bushes brimming with whistling
Blackbirds and the sun of October
Summery
25   On the hill's shoulder,
Here were fond climates and sweet singers suddenly
Come in the morning where I wandered and listened
To the rain wringing
Wind blow cold
30   In the wood faraway under me.

Pale rain over the dwindling harbour
And over the sea wet church the size of a snail
  With its horns through mist and the castle
      Brown as owls
35   But all the gardens
Of spring and summer were blooming in the tall tales
Beyond the border and under the lark full cloud.
      There could I marvel
      My birthday
40   Away but the weather turned around.

It turned away from the blithe country
And down the other air and the blue altered sky
  Streamed again a wonder of summer
      With apples
45   Pears and red currants
And I saw in the turning so clearly a child's
Forgotten mornings when he walked with his mother
      Through the parables
      Of sun light
50   And the legends of the green chapels

And the twice told fields of infancy
That his tears burned my cheeks and his heart moved in mine.
  These were the woods the river and sea
      Where a boy
55   In the listening
Summertime of the dead whispered the truth of his joy
To the trees and the stones and the fish in the tide.
      And the mystery
      Sang alive
60   Still in the water and singingbirds.

And there could I marvel my birthday
Away but the weather turned around. And the true
   Joy of the long dead child sang burning
       In the sun.
65   It was my thirtieth
Year to heaven stood there then in the summer noon
Though the town below lay leaved with October blood.
      O may my heart's truth
       Still be sung
70   On this high hill in a year's turning.

55 The conversation of prayers

The conversation of prayers about to be said
By the child going to bed and the man on the stairs
Who climbs to his dying love in her high room,
The one not caring to whom in his sleep he will move
5 And the other full of tears that she will be dead,

Turns in the dark on the sound they know will arise
Into the answering skies from the green ground,
From the man on the stairs and the child by his bed.
The sound about to be said in the two prayers
10 For the sleep in a safe land and the love who dies

Will be the same grief flying. Whom shall they calm?
Shall the child sleep unharmed or the man be crying?
The conversation of prayers about to be said
Turns on the quick and the dead, and the man on the stairs
15 Tonight shall find no dying but alive and warm

In the fire of his care his love in the high room.
And the child not caring to whom he climbs his prayer
Shall drown in a grief as deep as his true grave,
And mark the dark eyed wave, through the eyes of sleep,
20   Dragging him up the stairs to one who lies dead.

56 *A Refusal to Mourn the Death, by Fire,*
of a Child in London

Never until the mankind making
Bird beast and flower
Fathering and all humbling darkness
Tells with silence the last light breaking
5   And the still hour
Is come of the sea tumbling in harness

And I must enter again the round
Zion of the water bead
And the synagogue of the ear of corn
10   Shall I let pray the shadow of a sound
Or sow my salt seed
In the least valley of sackcloth to mourn

The majesty and burning of the child's death.
I shall not murder
15   The mankind of her going with a grave truth
Nor blaspheme down the stations of the breath
With any further
Elegy of innocence and youth.

Deep with the first dead lies London's daughter,
20   Robed in the long friends,
The grains beyond age, the dark veins of her mother,

Secret by the unmourning water
Of the riding Thames.
After the first death, there is no other.

57 *This side of the truth*
     (for Llewelyn)

This side of the truth,
You may not see, my son,
King of your blue eyes
In the blinding country of youth,
5   That all is undone,
Under the unminding skies,
Of innocence and guilt
Before you move to make
One gesture of the heart or head,
10   Is gathered and spilt
Into the winding dark
Like the dust of the dead.

Good and bad, two ways
Of moving about your death
15   By the grinding sea,
King of your heart in the blind days,
Blow away like breath,
Go crying through you and me
And the souls of all men
20   Into the innocent
Dark, and the guilty dark, and good
Death, and bad death, and then
In the last element
Fly like the stars' blood,

25   Like the sun's tears,
      Like the moon's seed, rubbish
      And fire, the flying rant
      Of the sky, king of your six years.
      And the wicked wish,
30   Down the beginning of plants
      And animals and birds,
      Water and light, the earth and sky,
      Is cast before you move,
      And all your deeds and words,
35   Each truth, each lie,
      Die in unjudging love.

58 A Winter's Tale

            It is a winter's tale
      That the snow blind twilight ferries over the lakes
      And floating fields from the farm in the cup of the vales,
      Gliding windless through the hand folded flakes,
5   The pale breath of cattle at the stealthy sail,

            And the stars falling cold,
      And the smell of hay in the snow, and the far owl
      Warning among the folds, and the frozen hold
      Flocked with the sheep white smoke of the farm house cowl
10   In the river wended vales where the tale was told.

            Once when the world turned old
      On a star of faith pure as the drifting bread,
      As the food and flames of the snow, a man unrolled
      The scrolls of fire that burned in his heart and head,
15   Torn and alone in a farm house in a fold

Of fields. And burning then
In his firelit island ringed by the winged snow
And the dung hills white as wool and the hen
Roosts sleeping chill till the flame of the cock crow
20   Combs through the mantled yards and the morning men

Stumble out with their spades,
The cattle stirring, the mousing cat stepping shy,
The puffed birds hopping and hunting, the milk maids
Gentle in their clogs over the fallen sky,
25   And all the woken farm at its white trades,

He knelt, he wept, he prayed,
By the spit and the black pot in the log bright light
And the cup and the cut bread in the dancing shade,
In the muffled house, in the quick of night,
30   At the point of love, forsaken and afraid.

He knelt on the cold stones,
He wept from the crest of grief, he prayed to the veiled sky
May his hunger go howling on bare white bones
Past the statues of the stables and the sky roofed sties
35   And the duck pond glass and the blinding byres alone

Into the home of prayers
And fires where he should prowl down the cloud
Of his snow blind love and rush in the white lairs.
His naked need struck him howling and bowed
40   Though no sound flowed down the hand folded air

But only the wind strung
Hunger of birds in the fields of the bread of water, tossed
In high corn and the harvest melting on their tongues.
And his nameless need bound him burning and lost
45   When cold as snow he should run the wended vales among

The rivers mouthed in night,
And drown in the drifts of his need, and lie curled caught
In the always desiring centre of the white
Inhuman cradle and the bride bed forever sought
50   By the believer lost and the hurled outcast of light.

Deliver him, he cried,
By losing him all in love, and cast his need
Alone and naked in the engulfing bride,
Never to flourish in the fields of the white seed
55   Or flower under the time dying flesh astride.

Listen. The minstrels sing
In the departed villages. The nightingale,
Dust in the buried wood, flies on the grains of her wings
And spells on the winds of the dead his winter's tale.
60   The voice of the dust of water from the withered spring

Is telling. The wizened
Stream with bells and baying water bounds. The dew rings
On the gristed leaves and the long gone glistening
Parish of snow. The carved mouths in the rock are wind swept
        strings.
65   Time sings through the intricately dead snow drop. Listen.

It was a hand or sound
In the long ago land that glided the dark door wide
And there outside on the bread of the ground
A she bird rose and rayed like a burning bride.
70   A she bird dawned, and her breast with snow and scarlet downed.

Look. And the dancers move
On the departed, snow bushed green, wanton in moon light
As a dust of pigeons. Exulting, the grave hooved
Horses, centaur dead, turn and tread the drenched white
75   Paddocks in the farms of birds. The dead oak walks for love.

The carved limbs in the rock
Leap, as to trumpets. Calligraphy of the old
Leaves is dancing. Lines of age on the stones weave in a flock.
And the harp shaped voice of the water's dust plucks in a fold
80   Of fields. For love, the long ago she bird rises. Look.

And the wild wings were raised
Above her folded head, and the soft feathered voice
Was flying through the house as though the she bird praised
And all the elements of the slow fall rejoiced
85   That a man knelt alone in the cup of the vales,

In the mantle and calm,
By the spit and the black pot in the log bright light.
And the sky of birds in the plumed voice charmed
Him up and he ran like a wind after the kindling flight
90   Past the blind barns and byres of the windless farm.

In the poles of the year
When black birds died like priests in the cloaked hedge row
And over the cloth of counties the far hills rode near,
Under the one leaved trees ran a scarecrow of snow
95   And fast through the drifts of the thickets antlered like deer,

Rags and prayers down the knee-
Deep hillocks and loud on the numbed lakes,
All night lost and long wading in the wake of the she-
Bird through the times and lands and tribes of the slow flakes.
100   Listen and look where she sails the goose plucked sea,

The sky, the bird, the bride,
The cloud, the need, the planted stars, the joy beyond
The fields of seed and the time dying flesh astride,
The heavens, the heaven, the grave, the burning font.
105   In the far ago land the door of his death glided wide,

And the bird descended.
On a bread white hill over the cupped farm
And the lakes and floating fields and the river wended
Vales where he prayed to come to the last harm
110   And the home of prayers and fires, the tale ended.

The dancing perishes
On the white, no longer growing green, and, minstrel dead,
The singing breaks in the snow shoed villages of wishes
That once cut the figures of birds on the deep bread
115   And over the glazed lakes skated the shapes of fishes

Flying. The rite is shorn
Of nightingale and centaur dead horse. The springs wither
Back. Lines of age sleep on the stones till trumpeting dawn.
Exultation lies down. Time buries the spring weather
120   That belled and bounded with the fossil and the dew reborn.

For the bird lay bedded
In a choir of wings, as though she slept or died,
And the wings glided wide and he was hymned and wedded,
And through the thighs of the engulfing bride,
125   The woman breasted and the heaven headed

Bird, he was brought low,
Burning in the bride bed of love, in the whirl-
Pool at the wanting centre, in the folds
Of paradise, in the spun bud of the world.
130   And she rose with him flowering in her melting snow.

59   Unluckily for a death

Unluckily for a death
Waiting with phoenix under
The pyre yet to be lighted of my sins and days,
And for the woman in shades
5   Saint carved and sensual among the scudding
Dead and gone, dedicate forever to my self
Though the brawl of the kiss has not occurred,
On the clay cold mouth, on the fire
Branded forehead, that could bind
10   Her constant, nor the winds of love broken wide
To the wind the choir and cloister
Of the wintry nunnery of the order of lust
Beneath my life, that sighs for the seducer's coming
In the sun strokes of summer,

15   Loving on this sea banged guilt
My holy lucky body
Under the cloud against love is caught and held and kissed
In the mill of the midst
Of the descending day, the dark our folly,
20   Cut to the still star in the order of the quick
But blessed by such heroic hosts in your every
Inch and glance that the wound
Is certain god, and the ceremony of souls
Is celebrated there, and communion between suns.
25   Never shall my self chant
About the saint in shades while the endless breviary
Turns of your prayed flesh, nor shall I shoo the bird below me:
The death biding two lie lonely.

I see the tigron in tears
30   In the androgynous dark,
His striped and noon maned tribe striding to holocaust,

The she mules bear their minotaurs,
The duck-billed platypus broody in a milk of birds.
I see the wanting nun saint carved in a garb
35   Of shades, symbol of desire beyond my hours
And guilts, great crotch and giant
Continence. I see the unfired phoenix, herald
And heaven crier, arrow now of aspiring
And the renouncing of islands.
40   All love but for the full assemblage in flower
Of the living flesh is monstrous or immortal,
And the grave its daughters.

Love, my fate got luckily,
Teaches with no telling
45   That the phoenix' bid for heaven and the desire after
Death in the carved nunnery
Both shall fail if I bow not to your blessing
Nor walk in the cool of your mortal garden
With immortality at my side like Christ the sky.
50   This I know from the native
Tongue of your translating eyes. The young stars told me,
Hurling into beginning like Christ the child.
Lucklessly she must lie patient
And the vaulting bird be still. O my true love, hold me.
55   In your every inch and glance is the globe of genesis spun,
And the living earth your sons.

60 In my craft or sullen art

In my craft or sullen art
Exercised in the still night
When only the moon rages
And the lovers lie abed
5   With all their griefs in their arms,

I labour by singing light
Not for ambition or bread
Or the strut and trade of charms
On the ivory stages
10   But for the common wages
Of their most secret heart.

Not for the proud man apart
From the raging moon I write
On these spindrift pages
15   Nor for the towering dead
With their nightingales and psalms
But for the lovers, their arms
Round the griefs of the ages,
Who pay no praise or wages
20   Nor heed my craft or art.

61 Fern Hill

Now as I was young and easy under the apple boughs
About the lilting house and happy as the grass was green,
    The night above the dingle starry,
        Time let me hail and climb
5   Golden in the heydays of his eyes,
And honoured among wagons I was prince of the apple towns
And once below a time I lordly had the trees and leaves
        Trail with daisies and barley
    Down the rivers of the windfall light.

10   And as I was green and carefree, famous among the barns
About the happy yard and singing as the farm was home,
    In the sun that is young once only,
        Time let me play and be
        Golden in the mercy of his means,

15   And green and golden I was huntsman and herdsman, the calves
Sang to my horn, the foxes on the hills barked clear and cold,
       And the sabbath rang slowly
      In the pebbles of the holy streams.

All the sun long it was running, it was lovely, the hay
20   Fields high as the house, the tunes from the chimneys, it was air
       And playing, lovely and watery
         And fire green as grass.
       And nightly under the simple stars
As I rode to sleep the owls were bearing the farm away,
25   All the moon long I heard, blessed among stables, the nightjars
       Flying with the ricks, and the horses
         Flashing into the dark.

And then to awake, and the farm, like a wanderer white
With the dew, come back, the cock on his shoulder: it was all
30   Shining, it was Adam and maiden,
         The sky gathered again
       And the sun grew round that very day.
So it must have been after the birth of the simple light
In the first, spinning place, the spellbound horses walking warm
35   Out of the whinnying green stable
        On to the fields of praise.

And honoured among foxes and pheasants by the gay house
Under the new made clouds and happy as the heart was long,
       In the sun born over and over,
40   I ran my heedless ways,
        My wishes raced through the house high hay
And nothing I cared, at my sky blue trades, that time allows
In all his tuneful turning so few and such morning songs
       Before the children green and golden
45   Follow him out of grace,

Nothing I cared, in the lamb white days, that time would take me
Up to the swallow thronged loft by the shadow of my hand,
    In the moon that is always rising,
        Nor that riding to sleep
50   I should hear him fly with the high fields
And wake to the farm forever fled from the childless land.
Oh as I was young and easy in the mercy of his means,
      Time held me green and dying
    Though I sang in my chains like the sea.

62 In Country Sleep

I

Never and never, my girl riding far and near
In the land of the hearthstone tales, and spelled asleep,
Fear or believe that the wolf in a sheepwhite hood
Loping and bleating roughly and blithely shall leap,
5   My dear, my dear,
Out of a lair in the flocked leaves in the dew dipped year
To eat your heart in the house in the rosy wood.

Sleep, good, for ever, slow and deep, spelled rare and wise,
My girl ranging the night in the rose and shire
10   Of the hobnail tales: no gooseherd or swine will turn
Into a homestall king or hamlet of fire
           And prince of ice
To court the honeyed heart from your side before sunrise
In a spinney of ringed boys and ganders, spike and burn,

15   Nor the innocent lie in the rooting dingle wooed
And staved, and riven among plumes my rider weep.
From the broomed witch's spume you are shielded by fern

And flower of country sleep and the greenwood keep.
                    Lie fast and soothed,
20 Safe be and smooth from the bellows of the rushy brood.
Never, my girl, until tolled to sleep by the stern

Bell believe or fear that the rustic shade or spell
Shall harrow and snow the blood while you ride wide and
            near,
For who unmanningly haunts the mountain ravened eaves
25 Or skulks in the dell moon but moonshine echoing clear
                    From the starred well?
A hill touches an angel. Out of a saint's cell
The nightbird lauds through nunneries and domes of leaves

Her robin breasted tree, three Marys in the rays.
30 Sanctum sanctorum the animal eye of the wood
In the rain telling its beads, and the gravest ghost
The owl at its knelling. Fox and holt kneel before blood.
                    Now the tales praise
The star rise at pasture and nightlong the fables graze
35 On the lord's table of the bowing grass. Fear most

For ever of all not the wolf in his baaing hood
Nor the tusked prince, in the ruttish farm, at the rind
And mire of love, but the Thief as meek as the dew.
The country is holy: O bide in that country kind,
40   Know the green good,
Under the prayer wheeling moon in the rosy wood
Be shielded by chant and flower and gay may you

Lie in grace. Sleep spelled at rest in the lowly house
In the squirrel nimble grove, under linen and thatch
45 And star: held and blessed, though you scour the high four

Winds, from the dousing shade and the roarer at the latch,
Cool in your vows.
Yet out of the beaked, web dark and the pouncing boughs
Be you sure the Thief will seek a way sly and sure

50 And sly as snow and meek as dew blown to the thorn,
This night and each vast night until the stern bell talks
In the tower and tolls to sleep over the stalls
Of the hearthstone tales my own, last love; and the soul walks
The waters shorn.
55 This night and each night since the falling star you were born,
Ever and ever he finds a way, as the snow falls,

As the rain falls, hail on the fleece, as the vale mist rides
Through the haygold stalls, as the dew falls on the wind-
Milled dust of the apple tree and the pounded islands
60 Of the morning leaves, as the star falls, as the winged
Apple seed glides,
And falls, and flowers in the yawning wound at our sides,
As the world falls, silent as the cyclone of silence.

II

Night and the reindeer on the clouds above the haycocks
65 And the wings of the great roc ribboned for the fair!
The leaping saga of prayer! And high, there, on the hare-
Heeled winds the rooks
Cawing from their black bethels soaring, the holy books
Of birds! Among the cocks like fire the red fox

70 Burning! Night and the vein of birds in the winged, sloe wrist
Of the wood! Pastoral beat of blood through the laced leaves!
The stream from the priest black wristed spinney and sleeves
Of thistling frost
Of the nightingale's din and tale! The upgiven ghost
75 Of the dingle torn to singing and the surpliced

Hill of cypresses! The din and tale in the skimmed
Yard of the buttermilk rain on the pail! The sermon
Of blood! The bird loud vein! The saga from mermen
                              To seraphim
80   Leaping! The gospel rooks! All tell, this night, of him
Who comes as red as the fox and sly as the heeled wind.

Illumination of music! the lulled black backed
Gull, on the wave with sand in its eyes! And the foal moves
Through the shaken greensward lake, silent, on moonshod
        hooves,
85   In the winds' wakes.
Music of elements, that a miracle makes!
Earth, air, water, fire, singing into the white act,

The haygold haired, my love asleep, and the rift blue
Eyed, in the haloed house, in her rareness and hilly
90   High riding, held and blessed and true, and so stilly
                              Lying the sky
Might cross its planets, the bell weep, night gather her eyes,
The Thief fall on the dead like the willynilly dew,

Only for the turning of the earth in her holy
95   Heart! Slyly, slowly, hearing the wound in her side go
Round the sun, he comes to my love like the designed snow,
                              And truly he
Flows to the strand of flowers like the dew's ruly sea,
And surely he sails like the ship shape clouds. Oh he

100   Comes designed to my love to steal not her tide raking
Wound, nor her riding high, nor her eyes, nor kindled hair,
But her faith that each vast night and the saga of prayer
                              He comes to take
Her faith that this last night for his unsacred sake
105   He comes to leave her in the lawless sun awaking

Naked and forsaken to grieve he will not come.
Ever and ever by all your vows believe and fear
My dear this night he comes and night without end my dear
                    Since you were born:
110   And you shall wake, from country sleep, this dawn and each
            first dawn,
        Your faith as deathless as the outcry of the ruled sun.

63   *Over Sir John's hill*

Over Sir John's hill,
The hawk on fire hangs still;
In a hoisted cloud, at drop of dusk, he pulls to his claws
And gallows, up the rays of his eyes the small birds of the bay
5   And the shrill child's play
Wars
Of the sparrows and such who swansing, dusk, in wrangling
        hedges.
And blithely they squawk
To fiery tyburn over the wrestle of elms until
10   The flash the noosed hawk
Crashes, and slowly the fishing holy stalking heron
In the river Towy below bows his tilted headstone.

Flash, and the plumes crack,
And a black cap of jack-
15   Daws Sir John's just hill dons, and again the gulled birds hare
To the hawk on fire, the halter height, over Towy's fins,
In a whack of wind.
There
Where the elegiac fisherbird stabs and paddles
20   In the pebbly dab filled
Shallow and sedge, and 'dilly dilly,' calls the loft hawk,

'Come and be killed,'
I open the leaves of the water at a passage
Of psalms and shadows among the pincered sandcrabs prancing

25   And read, in a shell,
Death clear as a buoy's bell:
All praise of the hawk on fire in hawk-eyed dusk be sung,
When his viperish fuse hangs looped with flames under the
     brand
Wing, and blest shall
30   Young
Green chickens of the bay and bushes cluck, 'dilly dilly,
Come let us die.'
We grieve as the blithe birds, never again, leave shingle and elm,
The heron and I,
35   I young Aesop fabling to the near night by the dingle
Of eels, saint heron hymning in the shell-hung distant

Crystal harbour vale
Where the sea cobbles sail,
And wharves of water where the walls dance and the white
     cranes stilt.
40   It is the heron and I, under judging Sir John's elmed
Hill, tell-tale the knelled
Guilt
Of the led-astray birds whom God, for their breast of whistles,
Have mercy on,
45   God in his whirlwind silence save, who marks the sparrows hail,
For their souls' song.
Now the heron grieves in the weeded verge. Through windows
Of dusk and water I see the tilting whispering

Heron, mirrored, go,
50   As the snapt feathers snow,
Fishing in the tear of the Towy. Only a hoot owl

Hollows, a grassblade blown in cupped hands, in the looted
    elms,
And no green cocks or hens
Shout
55   Now on Sir John's hill. The heron, ankling the scaly
Lowlands of the waves,
Makes all the music; and I who hear the tune of the slow,
Wear-willow river, grave,
Before the lunge of the night, the notes on this time-shaken
60   Stone for the sake of the souls of the slain birds sailing.

64 In the White Giant's Thigh

Through throats where many rivers meet, the curlews cry,
Under the conceiving moon, on the high chalk hill,
And there this night I walk in the white giant's thigh
Where barren as boulders women lie longing still

5   To labour and love though they lay down long ago.

Through throats where many rivers meet, the women pray,
Pleading in the waded bay for the seed to flow
Though the names on their weed grown stones are rained away,

And alone in the night's eternal, curving act
10   They yearn with tongues of curlews for the unconceived
And immemorial sons of the cudgelling, hacked

Hill. Who once in gooseskin winter loved all ice leaved
In the courters' lanes, or twined in the ox roasting sun
In the wains tonned so high that the wisps of the hay
15   Clung to the pitching clouds, or gay with anyone
Young as they in the after milking moonlight lay

Under the lighted shapes of faith and their moonshade
Petticoats galed high, or shy with the rough riding boys,
Now clasp me to their grains in the gigantic glade,

20   Who once, green countries since, were a hedgerow of joys.

Time by, their dust was flesh the swineherd rooted sly,
Flared in the reek of the wiving sty with the rush
Light of his thighs, spreadeagle to the dunghill sky,
Or with their orchard man in the core of the sun's bush
25   Rough as cows' tongues and thrashed with brambles their
         buttermilk
Manes, under his quenchless summer barbed gold to the bone,

Or rippling soft in the spinney moon as the silk
And ducked and draked white lake that harps to a hail stone.

Who once were a bloom of wayside brides in the hawed house
30   And heard the lewd, wooed field flow to the coming frost,
The scurrying, furred small friars squeal, in the dowse
Of day, in the thistle aisles, till the white owl crossed

Their breast, the vaulting does roister, the horned bucks climb
Quick in the wood at love, where a torch of foxes foams,
35   All birds and beasts of the linked night uproar and chime

And the mole snout blunt under his pilgrimage of domes,

Or, butter fat goosegirls, bounced in a gambo bed,
Their breasts full of honey, under their gander king
Trounced by his wings in the hissing shippen, long dead
40   And gone that barley dark where their clogs danced in the
         spring,
And their firefly hairpins flew, and the ricks ran round –

(But nothing bore, no mouthing babe to the veined hives
Hugged, and barren and bare on Mother Goose's ground
They with the simple Jacks were a boulder of wives) –

45   Now curlew cry me down to kiss the mouths of their dust.

The dust of their kettles and clocks swings to and fro
Where the hay rides now or the bracken kitchens rust
As the arc of the billhooks that flashed the hedges low
And cut the birds' boughs that the minstrel sap ran red.
50   They from houses where the harvest kneels, hold me hard,
Who heard the tall bell sail down the Sundays of the dead
And the rain wring out its tongues on the faded yard,
Teach me the love that is evergreen after the fall leaved
Grave, after Beloved on the grass gulfed cross is scrubbed
55   Off by the sun and Daughters no longer grieved
Save by their long desirers in the fox cubbed
Streets or hungering in the crumbled wood: to these
Hale dead and deathless do the women of the hill
Love forever meridian through the courters' trees

60   And the daughters of darkness flame like Fawkes fires still.

65   Lament

When I was a windy boy and a bit
And the black spit of the chapel fold,
(Sighed the old ram rod, dying of women),
I tiptoed shy in the gooseberry wood,
5   The rude owl cried like a telltale tit,
I skipped in a blush as the big girls rolled
Ninepin down on the donkeys' common,
And on seesaw sunday nights I wooed
Whoever I would with my wicked eyes,

10   The whole of the moon I could love and leave
      All the green leaved little weddings' wives
      In the coal black bush and let them grieve.

      When I was a gusty man and a half
      And the black beast of the beetles' pews,
15   (Sighed the old ram rod, dying of bitches),
      Not a boy and a bit in the wick-
      Dipping moon and drunk as a new dropped calf,
      I whistled all night in the twisted flues,
      Midwives grew in the midnight ditches,
20   And the sizzling beds of the town cried, Quick! –
      Whenever I dove in a breast high shoal,
      Wherever I ramped in the clover quilts,
      Whatsoever I did in the coal-
      Black night, I left my quivering prints.

25   When I was a man you could call a man
      And the black cross of the holy house,
      (Sighed the old ram rod, dying of welcome),
      Brandy and ripe in my bright, bass prime,
      No springtailed tom in the red hot town
30   With every simmering woman his mouse
      But a hillocky bull in the swelter
      Of summer come in his great good time
      To the sultry, biding herds, I said,
      Oh, time enough when the blood creeps cold,
35   And I lie down but to sleep in bed,
      For my sulking, skulking, coal black soul!

      When I was a half of the man I was
      And serve me right as the preachers warn,
      (Sighed the old ram rod, dying of downfall),
40   No flailing calf or cat in a flame
      Or hickory bull in milky grass
      But a black sheep with a crumpled horn,

At last the soul from its foul mousehole
Slunk pouting out when the limp time came;
45 And I gave my soul a blind, slashed eye,
Gristle and rind, and a roarer's life,
And I shoved it into the coal black sky
To find a woman's soul for a wife.

Now I am a man no more no more
50 And a black reward for a roaring life,
(Sighed the old ram rod, dying of strangers),
Tidy and cursed in my dove cooed room
I lie down thin and hear the good bells jaw –
For, oh, my soul found a sunday wife
55 In the coal black sky and she bore angels!
Harpies around me out of her womb!
Chastity prays for me, piety sings,
Innocence sweetens my last black breath,
Modesty hides my thighs in her wings,
60 And all the deadly virtues plague my death!

66 *An old man or a young man*

An old man or a young man,
And I am none of these,
Goes down upon the praying mat
And kneels on his knuckled knees
5 Whenever a fine lady
Does his poor body good.
And if she gives him beauty
Or a cure for his hot blood,
He weeps like one of the willow trees
10 That stands in a grave wood.

A wise man or a mad man,
And I am both of these,
Whenever a woman pleases him
With what she does not need –
15   Her beauty or her virtue,
Her sin or her honeyed pride,
Or the ice cold price she puts upon
Her white hot maidenhood –
Weeps like one of the willow trees
20   That stands in a grave wood.

Old or mad or young or wise,
And she is all of these,
Whenever a poor man needs her
She does her best to please:
25   For, oh, she knows in the loveless nights
And in the nights of love
That bitter gratitude is all
A loving woman can have –
And she weeps like one of the willow trees
30   That stands in a grave wood.

67 *Do not go gentle into that good night*

Do not go gentle into that good night,
Old age should burn and rave at close of day;
Rage, rage against the dying of the light.

Though wise men at their end know dark is right,
5   Because their words had forked no lightning they
Do not go gentle into that good night.

Good men, the last wave by, crying how bright
Their frail deeds might have danced in a green bay,
Rage, rage against the dying of the light.

10   Wild men who caught and sang the sun in flight,
And learn, too late, they grieved it on its way,
Do not go gentle into that good night.

Grave men, near death, who see with blinding sight
Blind eyes could blaze like meteors and be gay,
15   Rage, rage against the dying of the light.

And you, my father, there on the sad height,
Curse, bless, me now with your fierce tears, I pray.
Do not go gentle into that good night.
Rage, rage against the dying of the light.

68 from *Under Milk Wood*

[ELI JENKINS'S MORNING POEM]

The Reverend Eli Jenkins, in Bethesda House, gropes out of bed
into his preacher's black, combs back his bard's white hair, forgets
to wash, pads barefoot downstairs, opens the front door, stands
in the doorway and, looking out at the day and up at the eternal
hill, and hearing the sea break and the gab of birds, remembers
his own verses and tells them, softly, to empty Coronation Street
that is rising and raising its blinds.

REV. ELI JENKINS
Dear Gwalia! I know there are
Towns lovelier than ours,
And fairer hills and loftier far,
And groves more full of flowers,

5   And boskier woods more blithe with spring
    And bright with birds' adorning,
    And sweeter bards than I to sing
    Their praise this beauteous morning.

    By Cader Idris, tempest-torn,
10   Or Moel y Wyddfa's glory,
    Carnedd Llewelyn beauty born,
    Plinlimmon old in story,

    By mountains where King Arthur dreams,
    By Penmaen Mawr defiant,
15   *Llareggub Hill* a molehill seems,
    A pygmy to a giant.

    By Sawdde, Senni, Dovey, Dee,
    Edw, Eden, Aled, all,
    Taff and Towy broad and free,
20   Llyfnant with its waterfall,

    Claerwen, Cleddau, Dulas, Daw,
    Ely, Gwili, Ogwr, Nedd,
    Small is our *River Dewi*, Lord,
    A baby on a rushy bed.

25   By Carreg Cennen, King of time,
    Our *Heron Head* is only
    A bit of stone with seaweed spread
    Where gulls come to be lonely.

    A tiny dingle is *Milk Wood*
30   By golden Grove 'neath Grongar,
    But let me choose and oh! I should
    Love all my life and longer

To stroll among our trees and stray
In Goosegog Lane, on Donkey Down,
35   And hear the Dewi sing all day,
And never, never leave the town.

The Reverend Jenkins closes the front door. His morning service is over.

[CAPTAIN CAT AND ROSIE PROBERT]

One voice of all he remembers most dearly as his dream buckets down. Lazy early Rosie with the flaxen thatch, whom he shared with Tom-Fred the donkeyman and many another seaman, clearly and near to him speaks from the bedroom of her dust. In that gulf and haven, fleets by the dozen have anchored for the little heaven of the night; but she speaks to Captain napping Cat alone. Mrs Probert –

ROSIE PROBERT
From Duck Lane, Jack. Quack twice and ask for Rosie –

is the one love of his sea-life that was sardined with women.

ROSIE PROBERT [Softly]
What seas did you see,
Tom Cat, Tom Cat,
In your sailoring days
Long long ago?
5   What sea beasts were
In the wavery green
When you were my master?

CAPTAIN CAT
I'll tell you the truth.
Seas barking like seals,
10   Blue seas and green,
Seas covered with eels
And mermen and whales.

ROSIE PROBERT

What seas did you sail
Old whaler when
On the blubbery waves
Between Frisco and Wales
You were my bosun?

CAPTAIN CAT

As true as I'm here dear
You Tom Cat's tart
You landlubber Rosie
You cosy love
My easy as easy
My true sweetheart,
Seas green as a bean
Seas gliding with swans
In the seal-barking moon.

ROSIE PROBERT

What seas were rocking
My little deck hand
My favourite husband
In your seaboots and hunger
My duck my whaler
My honey my daddy
My pretty sugar sailor
With my name on your belly
When you were a boy
Long long ago?

CAPTAIN CAT

I'll tell you no lies.
The only sea I saw
Was the seesaw sea
With you riding on it.
Lie down, lie easy.
Let me shipwreck in your thighs.

ROSIE PROBERT
Knock twice, Jack,
At the door of my grave
45   And ask for Rosie.

CAPTAIN CAT
Rosie Probert.

ROSIE PROBERT
Remember her.
She is forgetting.
The earth which filled her mouth
50   Is vanishing from her.
Remember me.
I have forgotten you.
I am going into the darkness of the darkness for ever.
I have forgotten that I was ever born.

CHILD
Look,

says a child to her mother as they pass by the window of Schooner
House,

Captain Cat is crying.

69 *Poem on his Birthday*

In the mustardseed sun,
By full tilt river and switchback sea
    Where the cormorants scud,
In his house on stilts high among beaks
5   And palavers of birds

This sandgrain day in the bent bay's grave
   He celebrates and spurns
His driftwood thirty-fifth wind turned age;
   Herons spire and spear.

10   Under and round him go
Flounders, gulls, on their cold, dying trails,
   Doing what they are told,
Curlews aloud in the congered waves
   Work at their ways to death,
15 And the rhymer in the long tongued room,
   Who tolls his birthday bell,
Tolls towards the ambush of his wounds;
   Herons, steeple stemmed, bless.

    In the thistledown fall,
20 He sings towards anguish; finches fly
   In the claw tracks of hawks
On a seizing sky; small fishes glide
   Through wynds and shells of drowned
Ship towns to pastures of otters. He
25   In his slant, racking house
And the hewn coils of his trade perceives
   Herons walk in their shroud,

    The livelong river's robe
Of minnows wreathing around their prayer;
30   And far at sea he knows,
Who slaves to his crouched, eternal end
   Under a serpent cloud,
Dolphins dive in their turnturtle dust,
   The rippled seals streak down
35 To kill and their own tide daubing blood
   Slides good in the sleek mouth.

In a cavernous, swung
Wave's silence, wept white angelus knells.
   Thirty-five bells sing struck
40 On skull and scar where his loves lie wrecked,
   Steered by the falling stars.
And tomorrow weeps in a blind cage
   Terror will rage apart
Before chains break to a hammer flame
45   And love unbolts the dark

   And freely he goes lost
In the unknown, famous light of great
   And fabulous, dear God.
Dark is a way and light is a place,
50   Heaven that never was
Nor will be ever is always true,
   And, in that brambled void,
Plenty as blackberries in the woods
   The dead grow for His joy.

55   There he might wander bare
With the spirits of the horseshoe bay
   Or the stars' seashore dead,
Marrow of eagles, the roots of whales
   And wishbones of wild geese,
60 With blessed, unborn God and His Ghost,
   And every soul His priest,
Gulled and chanter in young Heaven's fold
   Be at cloud quaking peace,

   But dark is a long way.
65 He, on the earth of the night, alone
   With all the living, prays,
Who knows the rocketing wind will blow
   The bones out of the hills,

And the scythed boulders bleed, and the last
70   Rage shattered waters kick
Masts and fishes to the still quick stars,
        Faithlessly unto Him

        Who is the light of old
And air shaped Heaven where souls grow wild
75   As horses in the foam:
Oh, let me midlife mourn by the shrined
        And druid herons' vows
The voyage to ruin I must run,
        Dawn ships clouted aground,
80   Yet, though I cry with tumbledown tongue,
        Count my blessings aloud:

        Four elements and five
Senses, and man a spirit in love
        Tangling through this spun slime
85   To his nimbus bell cool kingdom come
        And the lost, moonshine domes,
And the sea that hides his secret selves
        Deep in its black, base bones,
Lulling of spheres in the seashell flesh,
90   And this last blessing most,

        That the closer I move
To death, one man through his sundered hulks,
        The louder the sun blooms
And the tusked, ramshackling sea exults;
95   And every wave of the way
And gale I tackle, the whole world then
        With more triumphant faith
Than ever was since the world was said
        Spins its morning of praise,

100 I hear the bouncing hills
  Grow larked and greener at berry brown
   Fall and the dew larks sing
  Taller this thunderclap spring, and how
   More spanned with angels ride
105 The mansouled fiery islands! Oh,
   Holier then their eyes,
  And my shining men no more alone
   As I sail out to die.

Notes

(Words or phrases quoted from the poems being annotated are always *italicized*. Paraphrases or quotations from other sources are in inverted commas. Letters, identified by recipient, month and year, are quoted from *The Collected Letters*, ed. Paul Ferris, Dent, 1999. *The Notebook Poems 1930–1934*, the main source of dating for the earlier poems, have been edited by Ralph Maud, Dent, 1989.)

1 Prologue (March–September 1952) 'It was going to be a piece of doggerel written to someone in the States on my return from there to Wales, but soon grew involved and eventually serious' (to Oscar Williams, March 1953). What it grew into was a prologue to replace the prose preface promised to Dent for his *Collected Poems* of 1952. 'I hope the Prologue *does* read as a prologue, and not as just another poem. I think – though I am too near it now to be any judge – that it *does* do what it sets out to do: addresses the readers, the "strangers", with a flourish, and fanfare, and makes clear, or tries to make clear, the position of one writer in a world "at poor peace" ' (to E. F. Bozman at Dent's, September 1952). So *this rumpus of shapes* (line 37) dedicates the *Collected Poems* (*these seathumbed leaves*, line 29). But it is itself an intricate poem. The first and last lines rhyme, and so on inwards until the exact centre of the poem (lines 51 and 52) is a rhyming couplet. 'Why I acrosticked myself like this, don't ask me,' he told Bozman.

Lines 19–20, **the cities of nine/Days' night**: A mixture of James Thomson's title *The City of Dreadful Night* (expressing Thomas's view of London and of American cities) and the idiom 'a nine days' wonder'.

Line 56, **deer**: In the old sense of 'beasts' (cf. *King Lear*, III, iv, 142).

Line 57, **bryn**: Welsh for 'hill'.

Lines 46–9 involve images of nuclear war, frequent in the late poems.

2 The spire cranes (Notebook version January 1931) 'Just a curious thought said quickly' (to Vernon Watkins, November 1937). It is, however, more a quick thought said curiously. The spire is a metaphor for the poet, the carved birds for poems so highly crafted (or so private) that they do not escape into the outside world but *jump back/To the built voice*. The *chimes* and the real birds represent a looser (and more communicating?) kind of poetry that does escape from the poet-spire.

Line 3, *carved*: Thomas defended himself against a remark by Stephen Spender by saying 'My poems *are* formed; they are not turned on like a tap at all . . . the last thing they do is flow; they are much rather hewn' (to Henry Treece, May 1938).

Line 4, *the spilt sky*: An image for water.

Line 6, *that priest, water*: Evoking Keats's 'Bright star' sonnet: 'waters at their priestlike task/ Of pure ablution round earth's human shores'.

3 Out of the sighs (Notebook version June–July 1932) The idea of disappointment in love is merged with a more general disaffection with life, causing the speaker to settle with stoic realism for a dog's life of small rewards – the *crumbs* of small comfort, the *barn* of mean housing and the *halter* by which horses are led – and people hanged.

Lines 7–9: The syntax is '*There must*, [God] *be praised,* [be] *some certainty,/ If not* [the certainty] *of loving well, then* [that of] *not* [loving well].'

Lines 10–11: Cf. 'Cowards die many times before their deaths.'

4 Their faces shone under some radiance (February 1933) A deleted title in the February 1933 Notebook was 'In Hyde Park', and the poem might be compared to Thomas Hardy's 'Beyond the Last Lamp (Near Tooting Common)'. It was the period of Thomas's first visits to London.

Line 14, *suicides*: 'The state was a murderer, and every country in this rumour-ridden world, peopled by the unsuccessful suicides left over by the four mad years [of war] is branded like Cain across the forehead' (to Pamela Hansford Johnson, Armistice Day, 1933).

5 I have longed to move away (Notebook version March 1933) Escape from social and religious conventions, which Thomas considered as bogus as nightmares, figures prominently in his early letters and prose. 'I shall have to get out soon or there will be no need. I'm sick, and this bloody country's killing me' (to Pamela Hansford Johnson, October 1933). But there is the worry (lines 11–14) that what may now seem merely the dead conventions of the home he wants to leave could burst into life, with an impressiveness that he has simply misunderstood.

Line 7, *salutes*: Ordinary social courtesies, parodies of communication.
Line 16, ***The parting of hat from hair***: The idea both of hair standing on end from fright and of hats raised in polite gesture.
Line 17, *receiver*: Telephone receiver.

6 And death shall have no dominion (Notebook version April 1933) Thomas's first publication in the London press, written in competition with his Swansea friend, Bert Trick, to produce a poem on the theme of 'Immortality'. Thomas's poem is more pantheistic than Christian, affirming a belief not in individual resurrection but in the indissolubility of the fact of life itself. The line opening and closing each stanza echoes a verse in St Paul's Epistle to the Romans (6:9): 'Christ being raised from the dead dieth no more; death hath no more dominion over him' – just as lines 7 and 11–12 echo Revelation (20:13): 'And the sea gave up the dead which were in it.'

Line 3, ***With the man in the wind and the west moon***: An interchange of 'the man in the moon' and 'the west wind'.
Line 14, ***Strapped to a wheel***: St Catherine was killed on a spiked wheel.
Line 25, ***hammer through daisies***: Cf. the common phrase 'pushing up daisies'.

7 We lying by seasand (Notebook version May 1933) 'I often go down in the mornings to the furthest point of Gower – the village of Rhossilli – and stay there until evening. The bay is the wildest, bleakest, and barrennest I know – four or five miles of yellow coldness going away into the distance of the sea. And the Worm, a seaworm of rock pointing into the channel, is the very promontory of depression . . . There is one table of rock on the Worm's back that is covered with long yellow grass, and, walking on it, one [feels] like something out of the Tales of Mystery and Imagination treading, for a terrible eternity, on the long hairs of rats' (to Pamela Hansford Johnson, December 1933). The poem itself is not naturalistic in that way, but a piece of mood-music possibly inspired by that scene.

8 Find meat on bones (Notebook version July 1933) Thomas's plea to his father in a more famous later poem, not to go 'gentle into that good night', also figures here, expressed this time by the father. But here it is counterbalanced by the son's opposite point of view. The father enjoins the son sexually to make most of time (stanza 1) and to *rebel* against the facts of life and death (stanza 2). In the remaining three stanzas the son, having followed the father's advice (stanza 3), replies that the very fact of death and the need for a sensitive life of the spirit themselves *rebel* against such advice (stanza 4). In the face of the inexorable, even if neutral, facts of existence the son enjoins the father to *take back* his words of revolt (final stanza).

Line 8, *ram rose*: Combining ram[bling] and ram[ming] – though Thomas had thought, mistakenly, that an older meaning of *ram* was 'red' (to Desmond Hawkins, March 1936).

Line 29, *Howls the foul fiend to heel*: 'Foul fiend' occurs nine times in Shakespeare's *King Lear* (e.g. Edgar's 'Bless thee, good man's son, from the foul fiend', IV, i).

Lines 30–31, *I cannot murder, like a fool,/ Season and sunshine, grace and girl*: Cf. Gerard Manley Hopkins's 'Spring': 'Have, get . . ./ Before it cloud, Christ, lord, and sour with sinning,/ Innocent mind and Mayday in girl and boy'.

Line 38: *War on the spider and the wren! . . .*: Cf. King Lear's 'The wren goes to 't, and the small gilded fly/ . . . Let copulation thrive' (IV, vi).

Line 40, *Doom on the sun!*: 'A Doom on the Sun' was the title planned by Thomas for an unfinished novel, in which anagrams of Lust, Greed, Cruelty, Spite, etc. appeared as the names of characters.

9 Ears in the turrets hear (Notebook version July 1933) Titled 'Dare I?' on its first publication in *John O'London's Weekly*, the poem is about the young Thomas's self-absorption in his private poetic world ('my islandic egoism' – to Trevor Hughes, January 1934). The seascape imagined in the poem owes something to the young poet's back bedroom in 5 Cwmdonkin Drive, Swansea, a steep street towering above Swansea Bay. Resisting Donne's truth that 'No man is an Island entire of it self', the poet felt that 'living in your own private, four-walled world as exclusively as possible isn't escapism, I'm sure; it isn't the Ivory Tower, and, even if it were, you secluded in your Tower know and learn more of the world outside than the outside-man who is mixed up so personally and inextricably with the mud and the unlovely people' (to Vernon Watkins, April 1936).

Line 9, **Hands, hold you poison or grapes?**: Suggesting a traditional visitor to a sickbed (the young Thomas was often 'ill' and securely pampered at home).

10 Why east wind chills (Notebook version July 1933) As in Shakespeare's *King Lear* (I, v, 27, 34 and III, iv, 152), the questions satirize the catechism form of some medieval texts. Nearer home, Thomas was once amused by his Swansea friend Bert Trick's young daughter innocently asking, 'What colour is glory?' The basic futility of such questions points up the folly of seeking intellectual explanations of what must remain a mysterious universe.

Line 2, **windwell**: Evoking Aeolus's cave of winds in classical mythology.
Line 11, **comet**: An image for a metaphysical answer coming down into man's hands, echoing John Donne's poem 'Go, and catch a falling star . . .', a similar attack on a futile need to know.
Line 20, **till the stars go out**: Cf. Donne's *A Funeral Elegy*: 'they doubt,/ Argue, and agree not, till those stars go out'.

11 The hand that signed the paper (Notebook version August 1933) In a particularly political decade for poetry, this is the only poem by Thomas on an overtly political subject. Its anatomical emphasis still makes it very different from, say, W. H. Auden's later 'Epitaph on a Tyrant' (1939). But behind it lies the openly political feeling of the poet's letters at the time. He pointed out that in the Great War 'French and German were shelling each other with ammunition provided by the same firm, a firm in which English clergymen and politicians, French ambassadors and German business men, all had a great deal of money invested' (to Pamela Hansford Johnson, January 1934). Arms deals were as much to blame as the political treaties that brought nations into war. 'Arms' may even be a hidden metaphor in the poem: *finger joints, hand, sloping shoulder.*

Line 1, **The hand that signed the paper**: Cf. 'The hand that sign'd the mortgage paid the shot', in Swift's 'Elegy on . . . Mr Demar, the Famous Rich Man'.
Line 4, **five kings**: The *five sovereign fingers* of line 2, where *taxed* also gives *sovereign* its financial meaning.
Line 10, **famine** and **locusts**: Along with modern political tyranny the poem evokes the theocratic tyranny of the Old Testament.

12 That sanity be kept (September 1933) The first of several poems chosen by Victor Neuberg for the 'Poets' Corner' of the *Sunday Referee*. Neuberg added that it was 'perhaps the best modernist poem that as yet I've received'. It reminds us of T. S. Eliot's 'Morning at the Window' and of the 'lonely men in shirtsleeves leaning out of windows' in Eliot's 'The Love Song of J. Alfred Prufrock'. Thomas wrote that the 'idea of myself, sitting in the open window, in my shirt, and imagining myself as some Jehovah of the West, is really odd. If I were some Apollo it would be different. As a matter of fact, I am a little person with much untidy hair' (to Pamela Hansford Johnson, September 1933). The poem had prompted Pamela Hansford Johnson to write to him in praise, thus inaugurating the most important correspondence of Thomas's early years. The poem also caused Stephen Spender to write to him.

13 Before I knocked (Notebook version September 1933) In a letter of September 1933 to Pamela Hansford Johnson, Thomas called this 'the Jesus poem'; but he often fuses his own and everyman's identity with Christ, and wavered in his use of capital letters even in this poem. The main drama here is in the fact that the speaker's consciousness predates birth, even conception itself (*and flesh let enter*, line 1).

Line 5, **Mnetha**: A name from Blake's *Tiriel*, where Mnetha's daughter, Heva, shared kinship with all things. *Mnetha* is also an anagram for 'anthem', 'the man' and 'Athena(m)'. Blake's illustration to 'The Gates of Paradise' shows a figure surrounded by a large worm, with the caption 'I have said to the Worm: Thou art my mother and my sister'.
Line 22, **snipped to cross the lines**: As soldiers 'snip' barbed-wire to 'cross' enemy 'lines'.
Line 39, **death's feather**: Cf. John Donne's *Devotions*: 'There is scarce anything that hath not killed some body; a hair, a feather hath done it.'

14 My hero bares his nerves (Notebook version September 1933) One of many early poems in which Thomas splits the human versus abstract or physical versus spiritual aspects of his created and creative make-up. The theme is poetry as a cathartic act. The body sees writing as a case of the *nerves* and *head* of the poet's sensibility and mind being *unpack*ed in an *unruly scrawl* on to the *lovelorn paper* by his *hero*, his alter ego. In line with other mechanistic images, the metaphor in the final line (*He pulls the chain, the cistern moves*) is that of flushing an old-fashioned water-closet. A further analogy is with masturbation (a Notebook poem of the same year contains the phrase 'cistern sex').

Line 12, ***like a naked Venus***: A reference to Thomas's favourite painting, Botticelli's *The Birth of Venus*, two copies of which he pinned on the wall of his writing-shed in Laugharne. Venus's heart-shaped face and *bloodred plait* of hair are seen as a heart with its emerging arteries and veins.

15 The force that through the green fuse (Notebook version October 1933) The poem that won for the poet, in a competition in the *Sunday Referee*, the publication of his first volume, *18 Poems* (1934). 'My own obscurity is quite an unfashionable one, based, as it is, on a preconceived symbolism derived, (I'm afraid all this sounds very woolly and pretentious), from the cosmic significance of the human anatomy' (to Glyn Jones, March 1934). The forces driving the inanimate world are the same as those governing the human body. The irony, however, is that man alone uses language – so 'dumb to tell' also means 'foolish to tell'. A letter to Pamela Hansford Johnson (December, 1933) parodies a poem of hers in which Thomas felt the same formula had been far too lightly undertaken:

> I am one with the steamship and one with the trolley,
> And one with the airedale and one with the collie . . .

> Though you talk all through of the relationship of yourself to other things, there is no relationship at all in the poem between the things you example. If you are one with the swallow and one with the rose, then the rose is one with the swallow.

Line 4, ***crooked rose***, and *crooked worm* in the final line, evoke William Blake's poem 'The Sick Rose'.

Line 12, ***quicksand***: Apart from 'sinking sands', the suggestion is of an hourglass, providing also the *quick* that completes the *lime* of line 15 as 'quicklime', the agent used to dissolve the bodies of executed criminals.

Line 14, ***hanging man***: Cf. the 'Hanged Man' of T. S. Eliot's *The Waste Land*, a figure in the Tarot pack, associated with the Hanged God whose sacrifice ensures the land's fertility.

Line 16, ***fountain head***: Metaphorically the womb, from which Time draws forth new life.

Line 20, ***How time has ticked a heaven round the stars***: Suggests that Time has made man invent Eternity (an earlier version read 'How time is all'). The image is also of a clock's face.

Line 22, ***sheet***: All at once 'flesh', 'bed sheet', 'shroud', and the 'sheet' of paper on which the *crooked worm* of the poet's finger writes.

16 In the beginning (Notebook versions September 1933 and April 1934) Though typical of Thomas's early interest in creationist themes, the stanzas are only illusively sequential (*In the beginning . . . And after came . . . Life rose . . . And from . . .* etc.) because they are in a sense interchangeable. Similarly, the poem's concern with the four elements is more a case of ringing the changes than of any ordered apportionment between stanzas (though stanza 3 contains all four elements). But this interchangeability suits the theme – that of inexplicable origins. An associated theme is the growth of language itself, from the original single Word (the *pale signature*, line 7, *three-syllabled* as is the word *beginning* itself) to the point where in the multiple words of human language it can later distinguish for the first time between birth and death (stanza 4). As Yeats put it, 'Man has invented death.'

Line 9, ***imprints on the water***: A reference to Christ walking on the water of Galilee (Mark 6:48–50).
Line 11, ***crosstree***: Technically, a horizontal brace on the head of a lower mast to support the topmast of a ship, but here both the tree in Eden and the cross.
Line 19, ***In the beginning was the word***: The opening words of the Gospel of Saint John (referring also to Genesis).

17 Light breaks where no sun shines (Notebook version November 1933) Thomas defended the by now expected similes of streams in the veins and lights in the eyes by saying, 'for the time at least, I realise that it is impossible for me to raise myself to the altitude of the stars, and that I am forced, therefore, to bring down the stars to my own level and to incorporate them in my own physical universe' (to Trevor Hughes, January 1934). But Thomas's mode is metaphor, not simile: he doesn't so much compare the human body with the physical universe as conflate them, dramatically elementalizing the human and humanizing the elemental. Though not in equal measure, the poem divides stanzas 1, 2 and 5 into a first part concerned with the living body and a second part concerned with death, whereas stanza 3 is devoted entirely to life and stanza 4 entirely to death.

Lines 1–2, ***where no sun shines;/ Where no sea runs***: i.e., internally, where *light* is consciousness and the *sea* is the circulation of the blood.

Lines 16–18: Thomas defended these lines against readers of the *Listener*, where the poem was first published, who had objected to 'the disgusting obscenity' of stanzas 2 and 3: 'The little smut-hounds thought I was writing a copulatory anthem. In reality, of course, it was a metaphysical image of rain and grief' (to Pamela Hansford Johnson, March 1934).

Line 16, *Nor fenced, nor staked*: The external forces that produce rain are unbounded, whereas the internal elements are held between *poles of skull and toe*.

Line 22, *Where no cold is*: Because, in death, notions of warmth and cold have ceased to matter.

Line 27, *When logics die*: At death, abstract thought changes into a new kind of physical sense: growth is no longer a mere idea but a case of things literally growing *through the eye*[socket].

Line 30, *the dawn halts*: 'Halts' in the sense of the old consciousness 'ending' and a new organic, pantheistic consciousness 'remaining'.

18 This bread I break (Notebook version December 1933) Written on Christmas Eve. Variations on the word 'break' link 'the breaking of bread' in the Holy Communion to the breaking of *the grape's joy* and the laying low of wheatfields to provide the elements for that ritual. Paradoxically, the life Christ gives in the eucharist involves the death of nature. The word 'break' was also there in the original title – 'Breakfast Before Execution', a version of 'The Last Supper' at which Christ inaugurated the ritual. Ostensibly spoken by Christ, the poem is both an expression of the central Christian tenet that new life comes from suffering and breakage and an ironic resistance to the urge to abstract significance from what is already a significant, living world. Thomas would have remembered Blake's claim in *A Song of Liberty*, that 'everything that lives is Holy'.

19 When once the twilight locks (Notebook version November 1933; thoroughly revised by March 1934) 'I'm enclosing one poem just finished. It's quite my usual stuff, I'm afraid, and quite probably you won't like it. But, honestly, the one "cancer" mentioned *is* necessary' (to Pamela Hansford Johnson, November 1933). The apology highlights the morbid tendency in so much of Thomas's early verse, from which the final stanza here is a call to escape. The poem is spoken by the more 'spiritual' side of a being that also has its more creaturely side. The first stanza describes the child when no longer a foetus closed in by the womb and when it has finished suckling. In stanza 2 he sends his own physical body (*my creature*) *scouting on the globe*. In stanza 3 the 'creature' spends only a short period in the ordinary world of common day, surrendering instead to the world of night and morbidity, and drowning *his father's magics in a dream*. (Behind this lies throughout, of course, the metaphor of the creaturely side simply dying.) Stanzas 4–6 image the kind of material represented by that morbid dream-world of adolescence. Stanza 7 summarizes the progress of the first six stanzas, and in stanza 8 the speaker exhorts his creaturely alter ego to awake and take full part in the ordinary waking world, where *worlds* of opportunity *hang on the trees*.

Line 3, **dammed**: Because the *twilight locks* of line 1 had *locked in* the amniotic fluid of the womb.

Line 12, **his rib** is that of the *creature* (line 9) which is a *globe itself* (line 10) in the sense of John Donne's 'I am a little world made cunningly/ Of Elements' (Holy Sonnet 2), which also makes the division between 'My world's both parts' (see above regarding the poem's speaker). At the time of writing the poem Thomas said, 'The greatest description I know of our own "earthiness" is to be found in John Donne's Devotions, where he describes man as earth of the earth, his body earth, his hair a wild shrub growing out of the land' (to Pamela Hansford Johnson, November 1933).

Line 17, **Drew . . . the straws of sleep**: The image of 'drawing lots' in a gamble is picked up later (line 40) in the phrase *by trick or chance*.

Line 19, **All issue armoured**: Though *issue* is a verb, it has here the force also of a noun in the army sense of items 'issued' to soldiers, thus completing the series *scouting . . . flask . . . fuses . . . charge . . . blew . . . powder*, and reminding us that Thomas was born at the outbreak of the First World War.

Line 24, **Christ-cross-row**: The alphabet, so named because a cross was placed before the alphabet in early hornbooks or spelling-books. It also suggests rows of crosses in a cemetery.

Line 26, **Sargasso**: A sea in the North Atlantic, between the West Indies and the Azores, full of floating gulfweed (*sargasso*).

Line 45, **pickthank**: Archaic for 'sycophant' and 'tell-tale', used by Shakespeare, Blake and Joyce – here described as *poppied* in the sense of 'drugged'.

20 A process in the weather of the heart (Notebook version 2 February 1934) William Empson wrote that Thomas had 'a very keen though not at all poisoned recognition that the world contains horror as well as delight; his chief power as a stylist is to convey a sickened loathing which somehow at once (within the phrase) enforces a welcome for the eternal necessities of the world' (*New Statesman*, 15 May 1954). Both external and internal life are geared to the interdependent *process* of growth-and-decay. This poem is even cooler than usual in its balancing of contraries, saluting Blake's statement that 'Without contraries is no progression' (*Marriage of Heaven and Hell*). The negative-sounding ending not only contains its own ambiguity (the *curtains of the skin* that death *pulls down* are in any case *shabby*) but is meant to round back again to the resurrectionist unfreezing of the tomb in stanza 1.

Line 5, ***their suns***: Can refer to both the *veins* of line 4 and the *night* and *day* (sun and moon) of line 5.

Line 6, ***the living worm***: An example of how the contraries are balanced even within one image: the *worm* of the grave is itself *living*.

Line 9, ***Drives in a death***: 'Incorporates death' in the embryo being born.

Line 12, ***unangled land***: Originally 'unplumbed'; one of the meanings is therefore 'unfished'.

Lines 14–15, ***half drops down . . . in a sleeping wind***: Combining the waste of windfall apples in an orchard with that of semen in wet dreams.

Line 20, ***Turns ghost to ghost***: 'Returns the uncreated to the decreated'.

Line 21, ***their double shade***: The shade of the two *ghosts* of line 20 – the nothing we come from and the nothing to which we return.

Line 24, ***gives up its dead***: Like bringing out the dead in a medieval plague, but with a contrary hint of resurrection.

21 Foster the light (Notebook version February 1934) A letter of January 1934 to his friend Trevor Hughes dealt with the experience of illness in both families. Thomas said that he probably escaped Hughes's kind of depression because of his 'islandic egoism'. Hughes replied: 'How shall a man die if he has never lived, or see the beauty of the stars through the lenses of his own darkness? For so many God has never lived, the faint glimmer within them the glimmer of their own mean ego. This dies upon them, and they must die in darkness; die in the night and move to eternal fields of darkness. Foster the light, and God be with you' (manuscript, State University of New York at Buffalo). Thomas was inspired by that phrase 'foster the light', but thought Hughes's God does not in fact obliterate other, darker aspects of our experience of the world. There is no real choice between light and shade, and the *nor* repeated throughout the poem means 'but do not'. Thomas develops points from his own letter that Hughes had perhaps misunderstood, most notably that Thomas's egoism is a serious belief in the equivalence between the microcosm of the body and the macrocosm of the outside world ('the flesh that covers me is the flesh that covers the sun').

Line 4, ***the snowman's brain***: A reference to Wallace Stevens's 'The Snow Man', depicting 'a mind of winter' that sees the literal outside world as completely other than itself.

Lines 13–14, ***the fly-lord's acre . . . a goblin-sucker***: Thomas's letter said that 'despondency' and 'the faults in oneself' can be 'too easily blamed on the things that go squawk in the night'; instead man must realize that, just as magically, his *wizard's ribs* also embrace the *heart-shaped planet*.

Line 16, ***the ninnies' choir***: Satirically, a heavenly choir of angels.

Line 28, ***O who is glory in . . .***: The syntax is 'O [may He] who is glory in . . .' The divinity that *gave these seas their colour* and *shaped my clayfellow* in the previous three lines is urged (line 29) *Now make the world of me* – just as the poet has made a microcosm (a *merry manshape*) of the macrocosm of the world.

22 Where once the waters of your face (Notebook version March 1934) A remarkably early poem on what in the second half of Thomas's career became an habitual theme – the loss of innocence and of a child's imagination. 'This new year has brought back to my mind the sense of magic that was lost – irretrievably, I thought – so long ago. I am conscious, if not of the probability of the impossible, at least of its possibility' (to Trevor Hughes, January 1934). The poem was influenced by the image of the Worm's Head, a promontory on the Gower Coast, the neck of which is alternately covered and uncovered by the tide, and a landmark that Thomas associated with visits with his childhood friend Trevor Hughes, himself given to tragic depressions. (See the short story 'Who Do You Wish Was With Us?' in *Portrait of the Artist as a Young Dog*.) The magically rich sea represents the optimistic wonder that one sometimes feels has faded from life, just as the dry sea bed conveys the death of the child's intuitions. 'And to begin, I want to believe in dragons . . . I want to forget all that I have ever written and start again, informed with a new wonder' (to Pamela Hansford Johnson, December 1933).

Line 1, ***the waters of your face***: A reversal of 'the face of the waters' over which the spirit of God moves in Genesis 1:2. The 'you' throughout is the external world that the poet inhabits.

Line 2, ***Spun to my screws***: The screws of a boat's propellers, but with the sense 'responded to my imagination', as in 'sang to my horn' in 'Fern Hill'.

Lines 16–17, ***the shades/ Of children***: The children who are no more, but who still yearn for *the dolphined sea* of the imagination (line 18). Cf. 'the childless land' in 'Fern Hill'.

Line 22, ***There shall be corals . . .*** : Cf. 'I become a greater introvert day by day, though, day by day again, I am conscious of more external wonders in the world. It is my aim as an artist . . . to bring those wonders into myself' (to Trevor Hughes, January 1934).

23 Our eunuch dreams (Notebook version March 1934) The cinema was an early and permanent passion, and its visual fictions one of Thomas's main sources of imagery. (It was the subject of a precocious essay, 'The Films', in his school magazine in July 1930.) 'There is no reason at all why I should not write of gunmen, cinemas *and* pylons if what I have to say necessitates it. Those words and images were essential' (to Pamela Hansford Johnson, March 1934). The theme was highly characteristic in another way: like the morbid adolescent dreams of 'When once the twilight locks' above, the glamorous but barren (*eunuch*) fictions of cinema deprive us of *faith* (lines 29 and 36) in the everyday world, the only one in which people really *flower as they love* (line 41).

Lines 1–3: the syntax is *Our eunuch dreams . . . Of light and love . . . Whack.*

Line 3, ***Whack their boys' limbs***: As principal-boys slap their thighs in the mock heartiness of pantomime.

Line 5, ***Groom***: i.e. '[Bride]groom', as a verb.

Line 12, ***love***: As a verb.

Line 14, ***swell***: As in both tumescence and a stylish showing-off.

Line 19, ***kiss or kill***: 'Kiss or Kill' was a childhood game like 'Truth or Dare'.

Lines 24–6, ***Pack off the shapes . . . the night-geared forth***: You have to decide to *pack off* (send packing) either the falsely respectable people of the daytime world or the false night-creations of films. Similarly, in lines 31–6, *This is the world* (cynically repeated) challenges us to decide whether the *lying likeness* of the cinema is not indeed the reality!

24 I see the boys of summer (Notebook version April 1934) One of the poems Thomas thought most highly of in *18 Poems*. It captures a mood expressed also in the letters: 'Life passes the windows, and I hate it more minute by minute. I see the rehearsed gestures, the correct smiles, the grey cells revolving around nothing under the godly bowlers. I see the unborn children struggling up the hill in their mothers, beating on the jailing slab of the womb, little realising what a smugger prison they wish to leap into' (to Pamela Hansford Johnson, April 1934). A friend recalled the young poet seeing, on the beach at Swansea, some middle-aged men in Corporation bathing-suits and commenting, 'boys of summer in their ruin'. The 'boys of summer' thus include adult members of the society around him, 'in their ruin' not only in the sense of being in decline but in that they prudishly suppress their natural sexuality. But it is likely that, throughout section I (though this is made specific only in stanzas 3 and 4), they are the soon-to-be-born embryos who will be tomorrow's adults. Birth involves a natural process that lays waste the richness of the womb, and the poet sees this as a foretaste of the anti-life attitudes of the adults the children will become. Though lamenting the fact, in section II he concedes that birth must proceed, but he does so cynically, as if he were himself now one of the dark 'deniers' (line 31), ironically celebrating that anti-life society. In section III he recapitulates the argument of the poem.

Line 1, *in their ruin*: Apart from the source given above, cf. Auden's lines in 'Consider' (1930): 'that distant afternoon . . ./ They gave the prizes to the ruined boys', with its source in Dean Farrar's *Eric; or Little by Little* (1858): 'May every schoolboy who reads this page be warned by the waving of their wasted hands from that burning marle of passion where they found nothing but shame and ruin, polluted affections, and an early grave.'

Line 26, *a chiming quarter*: The three months out of twelve that remain if birth does not take place, during which the unborn foetus would die.

Line 35, *Davy's lamp*: merging the miner's safety lamp invented by Sir Humphrey Davy and 'Davy Jones's locker', a traditional term for the sea.

Line 50, *Man in his maggot*: An image derived from the frontispiece to Blake's *The Gates of Paradise*, which shows a maggot with a baby's face.

Line 54, *kissing as they cross*: The *poles* are the phallic polarities of life and anti-life, reconciled in the inevitability of birth. At the same time they are the *poles* of two worlds – those of womb and world – touching *as they cross* and merge at the moment of birth.

25 If I were tickled by the rub of love (Notebook version April 1934) The last poem in the notebooks. Stanzas 1–4 relate to the four stages of life – those of embryo, baby, adolescent, and old man. If he were *tickled* (both sexually 'aroused' and 'amused') by the *rub* (the sexual sensation) of those stages of life, he would not fear the following: (stanza 1) the prohibitive theology that lies ahead in the myths of Eden and the Flood or the sexual turmoil of youth; (stanza 2) death at the hand of the law or in war; (stanza 3) the punishment promised for the sexual self-abuse of adolescence; (stanza 4) the passage of time or venereal disease. Instead, *the only rub that tickles* (stanza 6) – that moves him as man and poet – is a morbid fascination with mortality: *I sit and watch the worm beneath my nail/ Wearing the quick away* (stanza 5). As with Hamlet, this diseased obsession has unfortunately become the very essence of his sensibility. Therefore the *rub* to fear (in Hamlet's sense of 'obstacle' – 'Ay, there's the rub') is not sexuality, or even death, but the morbid obsessiveness in-between. The 'rub' the poet would welcome instead is an engagement with full, contingent humanity. He prays that it become his subject-matter: *Man be my metaphor.*

Lines 8 and 15, ***Shall it be male or female?***: The choice of sex, at conception a matter of genetic lottery, is later chalked on toilet walls on which adolescents draw sexual drawings of men and women.

Line 25, ***sweethearting crib***: The talk of sweethearts, learnt by rote – like so much else, it leaves an old man cold.

Lines 23–8: Thomas has, as so often, separated the halves of familiar words and phrases: *lock . . . jaw, butter . . . flies, Dead . . . Sea.*

26 Especially when the October wind (October 1934) Originally November, the change to an October wind celebrates the month of Thomas's birth, one that even more *especially* prompted him to write poetry, though both months remind us of time and decay. There is another, more individual theme: 'When I experience anything, I experience it as a thing and a word at the same time, both equally amazing' (quoted in E. W. Tedlock, ed., *Dylan Thomas: The Legend and the Poet*, 1963, p. 54). This indivisibility of word and thing runs through the poem in phrases such as *the syllabic blood, the wordy shapes of women, the vowelled beeches, the dark-vowelled birds*, etc. The repeated *Some let me make you* shows the poet's desire to communicate the non-verbal (*neural*) reality of natural things outside him as strongly as the verbal life within him: after all, it is the *signal grass that tells me all I know*. But he is locked into language, with the result that the *syllabic blood* can *drain* only words (stanza 1) – *heartless words* (last stanza) because they have left the physical heart behind. The last stanza still yearns (mutedly now, within brackets) to communicate the physical as well as the verbal reality of Wales, though we are asked to listen finally, not to this present poem of words, but to 'the dark-vowelled birds'.

Line 8, ***syllabic***: An extra meaning comes from Thomas's strong syllabic word-count in patterning most of his poems. The present poem, for example, has ten syllables per line throughout.

Line 10, ***walking like the trees***: Thomas's first version was 'Men in the distance walk like trees': cf. the first words of the blind man cured by Christ, 'I see men as trees walking' (Mark 8:24).

Line 12, ***star-gestured***: With arms and legs outstretched.

Line 19, ***shafted disc***: The disc on the shaft of a clock's pendulum.

Line 20, ***in the cock***: Both sexual and '[weather]cock'.

27 Should lanterns shine (November 1934) Keats seems relevant, in both his theory of 'negative capability' (the ability to remain 'in uncertainties, Mysteries, doubts, without any irritable reaching after fact and reason') and his famous verse-letter to Reynolds ('and to philosophize/ I dare not yet!'), his decision to allow only 'a very gradual ripening of the intellectual powers'. The theme is a young man's need to remain open to experience, to avoid closing the mind in scientific or philosophical speculation. The first stanza pictures the opening of an Egyptian tomb and finding that the *mummy*, though embalmed and painted, crumbles in the light of real day. The discovery of Tutankhamen's tomb near Luxor in 1922 had long since made Egyptian funerary themes fashionable in both books and films. A later photograph shows Thomas and his friends Vernon Watkins and Daniel Jones acting out a scene from a film about an opened Egyptian tomb that they had seen in Swansea in the early days.

Line 2, ***octagon***: Because of the shape of the lamp's aperture.

Line 6, ***false day***: 'False' because it is neither the light of real day nor the day of resurrection.

Line 10, ***like head***: Referring back to the first stanza, where the opening of the tomb was a metaphor for intellectual inquiry. This dismissal of philosophies of *heart*, *head* and *pulse*, when too independent of one another, is echoed in a letter contrasting D. H. Lawrence's blood philosophy and Aldous Huxley's 'sermon of the intellect': 'While the life of the body is, perhaps, more directly pleasant, it *is* terribly limited, and the life of the non-body, while physically unsatisfying,

is capable of developing, of realising infinity, of getting somewhere, and of creating an artistic progeny' (to Pamela Hansford Johnson, December 1933).
Line 18, ***playing in the park***: Cwmdonkin Park, opposite the poet's childhood home in Swansea.

28 *from* Altarwise by owl-light: sonnets I–V The ten 'Altarwise' sonnets were written between the Christmases of 1934 and 1935. The sequence is probably the most difficult of Thomas's poems, especially in terms of working out a developing narrative through all ten sonnets. But Thomas said that 'though they are linked together by a certain obscure narrative, they're entirely self-contained' (to Denys Kilham Roberts, summer 1936). Yet even individually, and though they dramatize familiar aspects of the Christian story (the crucifixion and resurrection of the last three sonnets, for example), they are difficult to integrate. For one thing, they switch quickly between tonal extremes – the sexual and the religious, the sacrilegious and the devotional, the flippant and the momentous, the personal Thomas and the historical-mythical Christ. That last division also raises the problem as to who exactly is speaking, at what event, and for how long. The following abstracts offer guidelines to the rationale of the first five sonnets (more detailed annotation is given below).

Sonnet I: Christ, crucified and castrated by some originating power, appears to either the newly born poet or to Christ's own newly-born self in Bethlehem, and declares both his immanence (his *bed*, cradle and grave, is as large as the tropical expanse of the world, of *Capricorn and Cancer*) and his partnership in the world's sexuality (*Capricorn*, the goat) and its mortality (cancer). **Sonnet II**: The resurrected Jesus, speaker of the last two lines of the first sonnet, continues as the speaker of the whole of the second. He tells the newborn child that he grows upwards to the stars as on a ladder, the uprights of which are *the verticals of Adam*, but whose rungs are the *cross-bones of Abaddon*, the piratical ribs of the Angel of Death. That is, physical life is not only born-to-die but deadly. **Sonnet III**: Again, the whole sonnet is spoken by the resurrected Christ, now describing his Incarnation. When *three dead seasons* (spring, summer and autumn) on the *climbing grave* of the year had brought the world to winter (the season of the Nativity), Christ dipped himself *in the descended bone* of a human body come down to earth. **Sonnet IV**: The speaker in the octave is now the growing boy, either the poet or the young Christ. Growing in intellectual curiosity, he asks those abstract questions that can have no meaningful answers in a solid world. Retrospectively (within brackets) he admits that the questions are like *nagging the wounded whisper* and like *hunchbacks* to the *poker marrow* of the resurrected Christ. But the crooked question-marks also challenge the straight bones of exclamation-marks, exclamations such as *I am the long world's gentleman* of sonnet I. Thomas the young whippersnapper or Christ the young iconoclast are then answered in the sestet by the resurrected Christ's calmer emphasis on *Love* – in an image of an unborn child seeing, filmed on the wall of the womb, pictures of those whom he will love after birth, beings beyond his own egotism. **Sonnet V**: The first five lines are spoken by the poet as narrator, describing a corrupted and hypocritical form of Christianity, promoted by a card-sharping 'Western'-type Bible-thumping evangelist. He is a *fake gentleman* as different from Christ, the *gentleman of wounds* of the first sonnet, as general western Christianity is from Christ's original teaching. The *fake gentleman* speaks from line 6 onwards, but the sterile surrealistic experiences that follow, including a surreal crucifixion-scene in frozen wastes, can also be taken as those of the youngster now under the *fake gentleman*'s influence.

Sonnet I

Line 1, **half-way house**: The tomb, half-way between life and death.

Line 3, **Abaddon**: (Literally, 'Destruction') the Angel of the Bottomless Pit (Revelation 9:11).

Line 3, **cracked from Adam**: An indicative past-tense verb, 'broke away from Adam'.

Line 5, **The atlas-eater**: 'What is this creature?' Thomas explained. 'It's the dog among the fairies, the rip and cur among the myths, the snapper at demons, the scarer of ghosts, the wizard's heel-chaser' (to Henry Treece, June 1938). Apart from its obvious meaning of 'a book of maps', an *atlas* is also the first cervical vertebra supporting the skull.

Line 6, **Bit out**: Thomas spoke often of 'a castrated Saviour' (to Pamela Hansford Johnson, November 1933).

Line 6, **mandrake**: Mandragora, a human-shaped root, with fabled powers of fertility, mentioned in Genesis 30:14–16. Because its scream was reputed to kill, dogs were used in its uprooting (hence *a dog among the fairies* and *bit out*).

Line 7, **penny-eyed**: Pennies were once used to weigh down the eyelids of the dead.

Line 10, **the windy salvage on one leg**: The one leg of Christ's cross in the storm on Calvary, and of his cross-pinned leg(s) on that cross, with *salvage* in the sense of 'what remains behind'.

Sonnet II

Line 4, **Weans on an artery the gender's strip**: Re-forming the castrated genitals of Sonnet I.

Line 5, **the short spark**: The moment of conception.

Line 9, **Rung**: Present tense – '(you) make rungs out of'.

Line 10, **Jacob**: A verb: '(you) ascend as on Jacob's ladder' (Genesis 28:12).

Line 14, **hemlock-headed**: Hemlock was the poison plant taken by Socrates in his suicide.

Lines 11–14, **Hairs of your head . . . wood of weathers**: 'The greatest description I know of our own "earthiness" is to be found in John Donne's Devotions, where he describes man as earth of the earth, his body earth, his hair a wild shrub growing out of the land' (to Pamela Hansford Johnson, November 1933).

Sonnet III

Line 3, **Adam's wether**: Adam seen as 'a castrated ram', the *butt* (target or object of ridicule) of the serpent that seduced Eve.

Line 6, **thunderous pavements**: Paradoxically, it was to a 'place that is called the Pavement' (John 19:13, where Christ was condemned under Pilate) that the fault in a pastoral Eden led.

Line 7, **Rip of the vaults**: Christ as 'harrower of hell'.

Line 9, **Rip Van Winkle**: The character in Washington Irving's story who slept for twenty years.

Line 11, **The black ram**: The Ram was the astrological sign under which the Incarnation took place.

Line 13, **rung**: Acceptable as past tense (instead of 'rang') all the better to evoke the 'rungs' of a ladder as well as the idea of 'ringing the changes' (i.e. inverting the upward movement on the ladder of Sonnet II).

Line 14, **antipodes**: Because in Sonnet I Christ described himself as sharing his bed with the southern tropic of Capricorn as well as Cancer; but also because the incarnated Christ was inverted in the *descended bone* of line 10.

Line 14, **twice spring chimed**: Christ was born as both God and man, and the Incarnation involved also a Resurrection.

Sonnet IV

Lines 11–12, **Love's a reflection . . . bread-sided field**: In Edith Sitwell's copy of *Twenty-five Poems* (1936), now at Texas, Thomas paraphrased as follows: 'Love is a reflection of the features (the features of those you will know and love after the womb) which are photographed before birth on the wall of the womb the womb being surrounded by food; a field being its own field, and the womb being its own food.'

Line 14, ***the cutting flood***: The image of *stills* from a film reel (l. 12) is continued. At birth, the pre-natal 'photographs' of future loved ones are *thrown back* (the opposite of 'projection') in that they are 'discarded' in a *flood* of celluloid on a cutting-room floor, but also because the umbilical cord is 'cut' after the breaking of the waters (*flood*) at the moment of birth.

Sonnet V

Line 7, **Ishmael's plain**: Abraham's son by the slave handmaid Hagar was sent into hungry exile in the wilderness of Beersheba on the birth of Isaac (Genesis 16: 21). The name Ishmael then evokes Herman Melville's *Moby Dick*, which in turn is merged with the whale in the Biblical story of Jonah.

Line 10, **snatched me by the hair**: In Melville's *Moby Dick* (ch. 78) Tashtego is snatched from the sperm whale's jaws by Queequeg 'boldly striking out with one hand, and with the other clutching the long hair of the Indian'.

Line 11, **Cross-stroked**: Cf. John Donne, 'Swim, and at every stroke, thou art thy Cross' ('The Cross').

Line 13, **where the white bear quoted Virgil**: St Mael in Anatole France's *L'Ile des Pingouins* (*Penguin Island*, 1908) has a vision of a white bear quoting Virgil's fourth Eclogue, the 'Messianic' Eclogue, with the phrase 'Incipe parve puer', traditionally taken to be a prophecy of Christ's birth.

Line 14, **our lady's sea-straw**: There is a weed called 'sea-straw', but the reference is also to 'our lady's bedstraw', a cross-shaped plant used with other herbs in cradles, and believed to have been in the straw in Christ's manger.

29 The seed-at-zero (Notebook version August 1933; revised March 1936) The very different Notebook version used the story of Joanna Southcott (1750–1814), a religious fanatic who claimed she was destined to bear Shiloh, the second Christ (Genesis 49:10; Revelation 12). Dropping that specific reference, the new poem turned instead to a range of military images (*zero* itself is 'zero-hour for attack' as well as pre-birth 'nothing'). It dramatizes the way in which the womb is impregnated, not by assault but by subtle fusion. This enables a religious, even Christian, tone to survive (e.g. in the image of *manna*, and the way in which a *humble village* brings the *hero* to birth while a continent and a hemisphere deny him). But the main concern is the birth of any human being. The stanzas are arranged in pairs, the second advancing only slightly on the first and linked especially by the interchangeability of the key words in their final lines (see first note below). Thomas employs a suitably unsettling music by imitating the rhythms of Longfellow's 'Hiawatha'.

Line 7, **manwaging line** interchanges with *warbearing line* (line 14) to produce 'man-bearing' and 'war-waging' (with similar interchanges in equivalent lines in the other stanzas); there is also the sense of 'crossing enemy lines' in warfare.

Line 16, **riddled**: 'As from a sieve', 'with bullets' (piercing the surface of the sea, as with pock-marking rain), and 'made into a mystery'.

Line 29, **labour**: Both in pregnancy and in 'working hard to support'.

Line 35 (and line 42), **sailors hide him**: As from Herod (Matthew 2:12).

Line 49, **Range**: In the sense of aiming weapons (the *cannons* of line 47).

Line 50, **Man-in-seed**: 'Run to seed', the opposite of *seed-at-zero*.

30 Then was my neophyte (April 1936) The unborn child in the amniotic fluid of the womb, a *neophyte* or initiate into the process of life, sees the course of its life projected by God on a screen under water. God, *the winder of the water-clocks*, is seen as causing the *horrible desires* of adolescence, the *green myths* of religion, the casualties (orphans, the deaf and dumb, the retarded) and the heartbreak caused by *Love's image* – even while promising that *'Time shall not murder you'*. But the *green and unborn and undead* child replies, *I saw time murder me.*

Line 2, **bent on its knees**: The foetal position in the womb.

Line 7, **My sea hermaphrodite**: As yet sexually indeterminate. 'Hermaphrodite' also applies to a ship (a brigantine) decked out with two kinds of sail.

Line 9, **bitten decks**: Combining 'hit the deck' and 'bite the dust'.

Line 25, **my vanity**: The Biblical 'emptiness of life' (Ecclesiastes 1:2) as well as personal vanity.

31 It is the sinners' dust-tongued bell (November 1936) Around this time, Caitlin Macnamara (whom he was to marry in July 1937) was in hospital for treatment for gonorrhoea. She said later that the source was not Thomas, but Thomas, too, had contracted the disease and may have thought himself responsible. A thread of images of disease (*claps, sulphur, foul sepulchre, crabbed, plagued* [originally 'clapped']) leads to the *urchin grief* of the last line, where the disease is *brought forth* in a parody of a healthy birth. The guiding metaphor of the poem is therefore that of being summoned to church by guilt (*sinners*), by fear of death (*dust-tongued bell*) and to something more like a black mass than a service of worship, marriage, or baptismal christening – though a version of this last does take place in stanzas 3 and 4. The stream of guilty images is backed by another, that of exorcism and excommunication, of 'bell, book and candle'. The church spire collapses and the ritual takes place undersea.

Line 13, *dark directly under the dumb flame*: An image Thomas got from a thriller he had been reading: 'the shadow is dark directly under the flame' (Vernon Watkins in a BBC radio broadcast, 5 March 1958).

Line 21, *the blue wall of spirits*: Thomas said this was to be seen as a 'sky full of ghosts: the curving crowded world above the new child', but with a suggestion also of the side of a chemist's bowl of coloured spirit: 'I *saw* that too and a child climbing up it' (to Desmond Hawkins, August 1939). The child is summoned by the *stone tocsin* (warning bell) of line 20, which is the sound that the spire's *bellmetal* makes in collapsing into the sea (line 12) and its metal weathercock in striking *on coral* (line 18).

Line 28, *a hyleg image*: 'Hyleg' is a term from astrology; hence the specific forecast of *nightbreak* as opposed to daybreak at line 26.

Line 29, *Nutmeg, civet* etc.: The sense is '[May] nutmeg, civet, and sea-parsley' *serve* as healing herbs to the *plagued groom and bride* (as Dylan and Caitlin will soon become) who have already *brought forth the urchin grief* of sexual disease. Cf. *King Lear* IV, 6, 128: 'There's hell, there's darkness, there is the sulphurous pit . . . Give me an ounce of civet; good apothecary, sweeten my imagination.'

32 How shall my animal (March 1938) 'I hold a beast, an angel, and a madman in me, and my enquiry is as to their working, and my problem is their subjugation and victory, downthrow and upheaval, and my effort is their self-expression . . . The new poem I enclose, "How Shall My Animal", is a detailed enquiry' (to Henry Treece, May 1938). The key to the poem is in that phrase 'self-expression'. The 'animal' of the poem represents the physical energies inside the poet which he seeks to bring to light but which are killed at the very point of their translation into language, which 'Lops, as a bush plumed with flames, the rant of the fierce eye,/ Clips short the gesture of [real] breath' (lines 38–9).

Line 4, *the spelling wall*: The poet's mouth.

Line 14, **_lionhead_**: A word suggested by Vernon Watkins, deriving from Revelation 9.17: 'The heads of the horses were like lions' heads'.

Lines 34–6: The images hark back to the way the biblical Samson was deprived of his strength: *shorn . . . sly scissors . . . thicket of strength . . . pillars.*

Line 44, **_in my breast_**: i.e. without emerging as its own self through *the wrackspiked maiden mouth* of language (line 37).

33 After the funeral (In memory of Ann Jones) (March–April 1938) Ann Jones was the poet's maternal aunt who farmed Fernhill outside Carmarthen, the location of the famous poem 'Fern Hill' (1945), celebrating Thomas's happy childhood holidays there in the 1920s and early 1930s. Ann Jones died in 1933, but Thomas's response then had been a short and cynically impersonal poem. Its rewriting in 1938 embraced a wider range of themes: the twenty-four-year-old poet was now reflecting on that first reaction at the age of nineteen. The hypocrisy of the mourners (lines 1–5) is now counterbalanced by the potential hypocrisy of his own inflated eulogy (lines 10–15), which he sets in contrast also to Ann Jones's simplicity (lines 16–20) and her puritan dignity in death (lines 31–5). Even so, in classic elegies even exaggerated praise is justified in its aim of bringing back to life things gone dead.

Line 2, **_muffle-toed_**: The hoofs of mules drawing the cart carrying the coffin were traditionally covered to muffle their sound.

Line 5, **_spittled eyes_**: Children sometimes put spittle on the eyelids in pretended grief.

Lines 7–8, **_slits his throat . . . sheds dry leaves_**: The hypocrisy of the younger poet's suicidal grief in 1933 produced only the *dry leaves* of an unsatisfactory poem.

Line 12, **_I stand_**: The poem's first main verb, the previous eleven lines being adverbial, governed by the opening word *After*.

Line 27, **_this skyward statue_**: Ann in this confessedly exaggerated elegy is imaged as a monumental carved figure on a grave.

Line 39, **_twitch and cry Love_**: From one of the poet's favourite books, Djuna Barnes's novel *Nightwood* (1936): 'if one gave birth to a heart on a plate, it would say "Love," and twitch like the lopped leg of a frog'.

34 The tombstone told (September 1938) A poem described by Thomas as 'ballad-like' and 'Hardy-like' (to Vernon Watkins, September and October 1938).

The odd story of a girl who died before the sexual fulfilment of her marriage-night is seen from different time-angles. The poet accidentally comes across her grave (line 5), sees that she had died before he was conceived (line 6), hears gossip about the story (line 16), imagines that, before he was born, he had seen her fate projected on the wall of the womb (lines 21–23), and, now at her graveside, hears the girl herself utter the pain of her story through the stone bird carved on her gravestone (lines 26–30).

Lines 29–30, *A blazing . . . his hair*: The image in the last two lines combines the idea of violent sexual intercourse with the imagined rough birth of a male child.

35 On no work of words (September 1938) The language of the opening lines is that of being on the dole (the tragic fate of the majority in the 1930s): images of opulence (*rich*, *purse*, *gift*, 'treasures') are set against their opposites (*lean*, *poverty*, *hungrily*, *expensive*). But not to have written poetry *for three lean months* makes the poet a culprit, not a victim, even at such a time: he has shirked his job, not lost it. His job as a poet was to return in artistic form the creativity he saw around him in the created world. The moral is in the difference between reciprocating the gifts bestowed (*to take to give*) and receiving them selfishly (*to lift to leave*).

Line 3, *my poverty and craft*: 'Poverty makes me lazy and crafty' (to Henry Treece, September 1938).

Line 4, *hungrily given*: Suggesting that God, who sent down *manna* to feed the hungry Israelites (Exodus 16), is himself hungry for a response: some of the Israelites refused the gift and the 'manna bred worms and stank'.

Line 5, *Puffing the pounds of manna up through the dew to heaven*: Cf. George Herbert's reversed images for prayer in the poem of that name: 'reversed thunder', 'exalted manna'.

Line 6, *bangs back on a blind shaft*: Because Thomas's *lovely gift of the gab* has been left unused.

Line 8, *will rake*: Death 'will call in the debts', like a cashier or croupier.

Line 8, *marked breath*: 'Marked' in a financial sense and because God 'marks' even the fall of a sparrow (Matthew 10:29); *breath* because it is poetry that is involved.

Line 11, *the nut of the seas*: 'The oaktree came out of the acorn; the woods of

my blood came out of the nut of the sea, the tide-concealing, blood-red kernel'
(to Desmond Hawkins, August 1939).

36 Twenty-four years (October 1938) One of Thomas's many 'birthday' poems,
paralleling Milton's sonnet on his own twenty-fourth birthday, 'How soon hath
Time, the subtle thief of youth'. Milton's lament for the first fast-vanished
twenty-three years is something Thomas dismisses within the brackets of his
second line. But both poets, with different visions, resolve to move forward with
a confidence that is in inverse proportion to any certainty that the future holds:
Milton's 'Yet be it less or more, or soon or slow' and 'To that same lot, however
mean, or high' becomes Thomas's simpler parting shot – *I advance for as long as
forever is.*

Lines 6–9: The governing metaphor (*dressed to die* [from 'dressed to kill'] . . . *strut
. . . money . . . town*) is of a young man going out on a date.
Line 8, **elementary**: 'Basic' and 'simple', but also suggesting the world of the
'elements' to which all lives return – the ultimate difference between Thomas's
and Milton's religious outlooks.

37 Once it was the colour of saying (December 1938) The sharpest of many
poems grouped together in *The Map of Love* (1939) self-consciously analysing
problems of Thomas's stylistic development. Against his early delight in form
over content, Thomas hopes to claim, like Pope, 'That not in fancy's maze he
wandered long,/ But stooped to truth and moralized his song'. (See Introduction.)

Line 1, **the colour of saying**: The aesthetic or rhetorical effect of words as
opposed to their denotative meanings. Cf. James Joyce in *Portrait of the Artist as
a Young Man*: 'He drew forth a phrase from his treasure and spoke it softly to
himself:– A day of dappled seaborne clouds. The phrase and the day and the
scene harmonized in a chord. Words. Was it their colours?'
Line 2, **the uglier side of a hill**: 'Uglier' than the open countryside the other side
of the suburban hill of Thomas's birthplace in Swansea.
Line 3, **capsized**: 'The size of a school cap' but also because the unusually steep
street makes the field opposite appear 'capsized', as on a sea.
Line 6, **the charmingly drowned arise to cockcrow and kill**: The realistic things
drowned under the charm of words will rise again and kill the old poet in him.
Line 7, **mitching**: Playing truant (West Wales dialect).
Line 8, **cuckoo**: 'Silly' or 'mad' (cf. 'they were old and cuckoo, sitting in the

empty shelter sobbing over nothing', a memory of the same park, in *Portrait of the Artist as a Young Dog*).

Line 12, ***my undoing***: The 'undoing' of his early style (cf. 'I must undo', line 5), the 'undoing' of the egotism of his early themes, and possibly his final 'undoing' as a poet if a new style proves unsuccessful.

Line 13, ***reel***: Both a fishing-reel and a reel of film.

38 Because the pleasure-bird whistles (January 1939) Thomas's third volume, *The Map of Love*, published August 1939, was in many ways a transitional one. Many of the poems in it, either new or reworked, were reappraisals of his old style and themes. The present poem was suitably placed first. Janus-faced (its original title was 'January 1939'), it too looks back – at 1938 – and wonders about the future. Hence the figure in lines 5–8, *on the tip* of the new year, refusing to look back to learn lessons from the past, and Lot's wife in lines 13 ff., who did look back at Sodom, only to be turned into a pillar of salt (Genesis 19:26). The opening image of the caged bird singing more sweetly when blinded with *hot wires* poses the question as to whether Thomas's own poetry would be better if he, too, suffered blindly by not looking back or not even trying to understand. What emerges, he said in a letter, 'is really a case for prayer' (to Desmond Hawkins, August 1939) – hence the *present grace* repeated over the *past table* in the last line.

Lines 1–2, ***Because the pleasure-bird ... sweeter?***: The myth that captive song-birds blinded with hot wires *sing sweeter* had found its way into a dream the poet had of a horse standing in a cage of red-hot wires, and someone saying 'He sings better now' (Gwen Watkins, *Portrait of a Friend*, p. 68).

Lines 3–4, ***Convenient bird and beast***: 'Convenient' since they simply have to suffer the meal (*supper and knives*) that he makes of them as symbols and 'food for thought'.

Line 5, ***sniffed***: Suggesting drug-taking.

Line 19, ***the mauled pictures of boys***: Describing as Sodom the London from which Thomas had just returned (a 'city of the restless dead ... its glamour smells of goat; there's no difference between good and bad': to Vernon Watkins, December 1938).

39 If my head hurt a hair's foot (March 1939) Prompted by the birth of Thomas's first child, Llewelyn, in January 1939. The first three stanzas are spoken by the unborn child, and the last three by the mother, salving the child's sense of guilt at causing her the pain of his birth. 'It is not a narrative, nor an argument, but a series of conflicting images which move through pity and violence to an unreconciled acceptance of suffering: the mother's *and* the child's. This poem has been called obscure. I refuse to believe that it is obscurer than pity, violence, or suffering. But being a poem, not a lifetime, it is more compressed' (Thomas, reading the poem on the BBC Third Programme, September 1949).

Line 4, **worm of the ropes**: The umbilical cord (coiled and therefore, in effect, plural) links with the ropes of a boxing-ring for the images that then follow: *bully, clouted, ring, duck* and *the ghost with a hammer* – the last being the popular description of the Welsh ex-miner Jimmy Wilde ('The ghost with a hammer in his hand'), fly-weight boxing hero of the 1910s and 20s.

Lines 16–17, **Christ's dazzling bed/ Or a nacreous sleep**: The painful birth contrasted with the miraculous birth of Christ and the slow chemical process that produces 'nacre' (mother-of-pearl).

Line 20, **host of waters breaks**: The first stage of birth is known as 'the breaking of the waters'.

40 To Others than You (May 1939) The title uses the old courtesy, 'present company excepted'. Someone along the line has, in bogus friendship, made Thomas lay bare his private feelings and then betrayed him. The poem satirically matches the deceit with its own jinking syntax, stretched out over a twenty-line sentence of, essentially, a one-sentence poem: *You . . . Whom now I conjure to stand as thief . . . Were once such a creature . . .* [That] *I never thought to utter or think . . . That . . . My friends were enemies on stilts/ With their heads in a cunning cloud.*

Line 1, **Friend by enemy I call you out**: 'Friend, I call you out by calling you an enemy.'

Line 10, **the memory worked by mirrors**: The poem itself: in the broadcast 'A Few Words of a Kind' Thomas described poetry as 'worked by mirrors'.

Line 15, **desireless familiar**: 'a phrase in my "Orchards" ['The Orchards', a story of the early 1930s] and what caused me to write the poem' (to Vernon Watkins, June 1939).

Line 17, **displaced a truth in the air**: i.e. by uttering a lie.

41 When I woke (July 1939) 'This war, trembling even on the edge of Laugharne, fills me with such horror and terror and lassitude' (to Vernon Watkins, August

1939). The poet is woken from his private nightmares (the *spoilers and pokers of sleep* of line 5) by the ordinary sights and sounds of the morning in Laugharne which *din aside, dispel* and *slash down* the terrors of night. But a *voice in the erected air* of a radio news bulletin announces a different nightmare – the now certain outbreak of a Second World War. In its original printing in *Seven* magazine in autumn 1939, the poem ended with lines that combined a fear of Italy ('bulls'), Russia ('wolves') and Germany (eagles' 'nests'):

> Shaking humanity's houses:
> Wake to see one morning breaking
> Bulls and wolves in iron palaces:
> Winds in their nests in the ruins of man.

A plague on all totalitarian houses, obviously!

Line 11, **double of Time**: The double of Old Father Time, who traditionally carries a scythe.

Line 14, **a wand or subtle bough**: Such as might lead the poet back into the world of nightmare.

Line 16–21, **Every morning . . . Everybody's earth**: The poet whose morning composure has been interrupted by the declaration of war has often played at being *God in bed*, inventing *good and bad*, imagining a miraculous walk on the water and marking the fall of not only sparrows (Matthew 10:29) but of the *death-stagged scatter-breath/ Mammoth*.

Line 30, **shells**: A reference also to bomb-shells.

42 Paper and sticks (Autumn 1939) An unusually 'realistic' poem for Thomas, which is probably why, having included it in *Deaths and Entrances* in 1946, he later omitted it from *Collected Poems* in 1952. An accomplished dramatic monologue, it belongs more to the world of the later prose and of *Under Milk Wood*.

43 Once below a time (December 1939) One of the few 'collected' poems to elaborate on the comic swagger of the 'young dog' persona that Thomas describes so often in the prose. He was at this time writing the autobiographical stories that comprise *Portrait of the Artist as a Young Dog* (1940). He came close to including the poem in *Deaths and Entrances* in 1946, but held it back to spend more time on it, bringing it into the *Collected Poems* in 1952. It expands the concentrated image of 'Twenty-four years' (October 1938, above): 'Dressed to die, the sensual strut began'. The idea of the flesh that surrounds the spirit being like a suit carefully and censoriously made by tailors is here linked also to what was most outlandish in dress and action in the poet's early bohemian self, in Swansea and London. The poem's maritime imagery also seems to capitalize for once on the uniqueness of his Christian name, Dylan ('son of the wave'), from the medieval Welsh classic, *The Mabinogion*. But now, four months into the war, newly married and a young father, he would happily settle for settling down, to *live/ As quiet as a bone* (lines 50–51) – though determined *never to regret* his early showmanship.

Lines 4–5, *serial sum . . ./ the first of each hardship*: An image from hire-purchase, with the premium due on the first of each month.

Line 21, *the kangaroo foot of the earth*: Thomas acknowledged that the reference was to D. H. Lawrence's poem 'Kangaroo' (to Vernon Watkins, January 1940).

Line 24, *the lubber crust of Wales*: With puns on '(b)lubber' and 'w(h)ales'.

Line 27, *Shabby and Shorten*: A parody name for a tailoring company: for some time Thomas thought of the poem under that very title (to David Higham, December 1951).

44 There was a saviour (February 1940) The poem dramatizes the radical Blakean view of Christ as a person betrayed by the organized religion founded in His name. It employs the verse form of what Kathleen Raine recalls was Thomas's favourite poem, Milton's 'On the Morning of Christ's Nativity'. 'The churches are wrong because they standardize our gods, because they label our morals, because they laud the death of a vanished Christ, and fear the crying of the new Christ in the wilderness' (to Pamela Hansford Johnson, November 1933). In a cold winter, in the first hopeless shock of the war, Thomas laments that individual moral responsibility for humanity has foundered in the escapism of an institutionalized church. The imagery draws on the overwhelming but non-military force of Christ's teaching: 'I did not come to send peace but a sword' (Matthew 10:34): e.g. *crueller than truth, that murdering breath, the tremendous shout, you sighed as he struck.*

Lines 4–5, *Children kept from the sun/ Assembled at his tongue*: Either early Christians previously denied Christ's presence, or modern children kept from (and out of) the sun in Sunday School, or *assembled* in school 'Assemblies'.

Line 6, ***the golden note turn in a groove***: The message taught either monotonously or by rote.

Line 8, ***keyless***: In contrast to the imprisoning *jails and studies* and *lairs and asylums* (line 16) that man has made out of Christ's message.

Lines 22–3, ***unearthly flood . . . cloud-formed shell***: Their pity and prayers went heavenwards (as also in *wailed and nested in the sky-blue wall*, line 31).

Line 25, ***blacked***: Both morally and in the sense of the wartime 'blackout'.

Line 30, ***near and fire neighbour***: Suggesting 'near and far neighbour', starting a series of phrases denoting people unknown for whom we still have moral responsibility: *the little known fall, homes/ That did not nurse our bones, Our own true strangers' dust*, etc.

Line 39, ***Exiled***: Love seen as exiled ('cut off') in each individual, and which we *arouse* in order to return again into the public world without clenched fists (*Unclenched*) and without armaments (*armless*).

Line 40, ***rocks***: The rock of cruelty, the rock over Christ's tomb, and the rock of the established church itself.

45 Into her lying down head (March–June 1940) 'All over the world love is being betrayed as always, and a million years have not calmed the uncalculated ferocity of each betrayal or the terrible loneliness afterwards. Man is denying his partner man or woman and whores with the whole night, begetting a monstrous brood . . .' (Thomas's note under the poem in his copybook). He said it was a poem 'about modern love' (to Vernon Watkins, June 1940) and even considered borrowing the title of George Meredith's long tragic poem *Modern Love* (1862).

Line 8, ***Whales***: Associated with rival lovers, as also in 'Ballad of the Long-legged Bait' below.

Lines 11–13, ***Juan aflame . . . in his hair***: Don Juan (the legendary Spanish nobleman and philanderer), Queen Catherine (Catherine the Great, of Russia) and the biblical Samson are all associated with sex and the betrayal of love; the stroke of genius was in including 'savagely young King Lear', from subtler intimations of Lear's early sexuality in Shakespeare's play.

Line 16, ***the dark blade and wanton***: The 'mysterious dashing young man' and the mere 'lecher'.

Line 20, ***the burning England***: At this time Thomas and Caitlin were living with her mother in Hampshire.

Line 23, ***laid***: 'Lay' in the sexual sense.

Lines 30–31, **Resembling . . ./ The thief of adolescence**: Caitlin had been raped in her mid-teens by the painter Augustus John, over six years before she met Dylan.

Line 51, **domed and soil-based**: This was 'helled and heavened' in the first version.

Line 53, **the female, deadly**: Playing on Kipling's claim (from natural history) that 'The female of the species is more deadly than the male' (*The Female of the Species*).

Line 59, **the treading hawk**: 'To tread' is a term for a male bird's copulation with the female.

Line 67, **A man torn up**: Thomas himself, distressed by the infidelities.

Line 68, **second comers**: Capable of more than one arousal.

46 The Countryman's Return (summer 1940) A poem on the contrast between his London life and the rural places to which he always returned. He saw the poem as a half-comic attack on himself and acknowledged the heavy hand with which it pokes fun at his middle-class poet's stance, the Whitmanesque 'grand delusions of all embracing humanitarianism' (to Vernon Watkins, March 1940). But, though finally uncollected, and in some ways a sport, it received Thomas's serious, even protective, attention.

Line 69, **A singing Walt**: A reference to the American poet Walt Whitman (hence 'beardlessly', line 72), with a pun on 'single malt' whisky.

Line 77, **Cut**: A cinema director's command to end filming, also cutting out the memory of London scenes now left behind, e.g. the *paper-blowing tubes* of the underground.

Line 92, **this anachronistic scene**: Because Thomas's retreats at this time (his mother-in-law's house in Hampshire and his beloved Laugharne) were rural and unmodern.

47 Deaths and Entrances (summer 1940) The title is from John Donne's sermon, *Death's Duell*: 'Deliverance from that death, the death of the womb, is an entrance, a delivery over to another death'. This 'poem about invasion' (to Vernon Watkins, summer 1940) addresses anyone on the *eve* of being killed or of having friends and neighbours killed in the incendiary bombing raids on London. After a particular raid, Thomas wrote, 'I get nightmares like invasions, all successful' (to Vernon Watkins, August 1940). The first stanza concerns the death of one of those you have best loved or always known and the second stanza those not known personally (*sun* [son] *of another street*), whether on your side in the struggle (a young RAF fighter pilot?) or a fighter on the other side. These are the *near and strange* of stanza 3 who seek *your single grave* as one still only on the potential eve of death. But the figure that will finally reach you is Death itself – because your *heart is luminous/ In the watched dark* of both general mortality and the monitored wartime blackout. Death is then imaged, close-up, as a German pilot crashing in the very act of killing you; hence the final reference to Samson. (The letter to Watkins describes a German plane brought down close-by in Tottenham Court Road.)

Line 33, **darkened keys**: The keys to private houses and private lives. But to Vernon Watkins the poet also describes visiting a bombed aerodrome where the only one killed was a man who had been playing a piano in a dark and otherwise empty canteen.

Line 35, **that one loved least**: However much one hates a wartime enemy, the enemy loved least of all is Death itself.

Line 36, **Samson**: Killed in bringing the temple down on his enemies (Judges 16:26–30), Samson was also mentioned in Donne's *Death's Duell* sermon which gave the poem its title: 'Still pray we for a peaceable life against violent death . . . but never make ill conclusions upon persons overtaken with such deaths . . . [God] received Sampson, who went out of this world in such a manner.'

48 Ballad of the Long-legged Bait (January–April 1941) Of the several explanations that Thomas offered of this allegory, some are more repeatable than others. But all point up the same theme. William York Tindall records this paraphrase by Thomas: 'A young man . . . goes fishing for sexual experience – though this is not quite how he put it; but the fisherman "catches the church and the village green"' (*A Reader's Guide to Dylan Thomas*, p. 260). Thomas also said it was 'a poem about a man who fished with a woman for bait and caught a horrible collection' (to John Davenport, January 1941). The theme of a wild young manhood tamed at last in marriage and old age figures in other Thomas poems (e.g. 'Lament'). The power of the ballad, however, comes from its brilliant marine and submarine descriptiveness. Vernon Watkins, who saw the growth of the whole poem, said that it 'was so much a visual poem that [Thomas] made a coloured picture for it which he pinned on the wall of his room, a picture of a woman lying at the bottom of the sea. She was a new Loreley revealing the pitfalls of destruction awaiting those who attempted to put off the flesh' (Gwen Watkins, *Portrait of a Friend*, p. 91). The ballad is in a lineage from poems such as Donne's 'The Baite' (with the idea of a girl as bait), Coleridge's 'The Ancient Mariner' (ending with a hermit and a wedding-feast), Matthew Arnold's 'The Forsaken Merman' ('And alone dwell forever the kings of the sea') and Rimbaud's 'Bateau ivre' ('The Drunken Boat', which Thomas would have read in his friend Norman Cameron's translation in *New Verse*, June–July 1936).

Line 32, **hilly with whales**: Thomas told William York Tindall that 'whales mean [sexual] rivals'. Like 'Into her lying down head' (1940), the ballad, too, is about marital jealousy: on a worksheet now at Buffalo the poet wrote 'Dylan and Caitlin'.

Lines 41–3, **He saw the storm . . ./ Fire on starlight**: Cf. *Othello*: 'The chidden billow seems to pelt the clouds;/ The wind-shaked surge, with high and monstrous mane,/ Seems to cast water on the burning Bear/ And quench the guards of th'ever-fixèd Pole' (II, i, 12–15).

Line 54, **Jericho . . . lungs**: The shouting of the Israelites brought down the walls of the city (Joshua 6:20).

Line 68, **bulls of Biscay**: Bull-whales in the Bay of Biscay.

Line 80, **with his tread of snow**: Cf. James Elroy Flecker's 'The Dying Patriot': 'Augustine with his feet of snow'; but 'tread' is also the term for a male bird's copulation with the female.

Lines 107–9, **Susanna . . . Sheba**: In the Old Testament Apocrypha two *bearded* elders spied on Susanna while she was bathing in a *stream*; and in I Kings 10:1–13 (the 'Song of Songs') Sheba, visiting Solomon, was awarded 'all her desire, whatever she asked', but the only *kings* attending her now are the *hungry* predators of the sea.

Line 147, **His fathers cling**: The poet's own forebears are among the things caught by the bait.

Line 159, **walked on the earth in the evening**: Having eaten of the forbidden tree, Adam and Eve 'heard the voice of the Lord God walking in the garden in the cool of the day' (Genesis 3:8).

Line 165, **divining land**: From here to the end, the poem doesn't so much return to land as find land deeper down than the sea, pressing home the poem's point that we always arrive at the ordinariness we thought we were escaping.

Line 191, **Sodom Tomorrow**: A play on Sodom and Gomorrah (Genesis 19:24).

Line 200, ***ox-killing house of love***: Parodying the killing of the fatted calf in the parable of the prodigal son (Luke 15:23–7).

49 On the Marriage of a Virgin (July 1941) The basic idea was there in a longer Notebook poem of March 1933, just before his sister's wedding in May of that year. But the condensed conceit of this unorthodox sonnet makes it stylistically a new poem. The girl's *virginity* was *miraculous* because she had in effect a *multitude of loves*. Her lover was only the sun but every morning when she opened her eyes he *surprised* (as a new lover does an old) his own *golden yesterday asleep upon the iris*. The girl is *no longer ... married alone ...* for now *a man sleeps where fire leapt down*. The contrast, linking above and below, is in the tradition of poems such as W. B. Yeats's 'Leda and the Swan'.

Line 3, ***iris***: Apart from the literal reference, Iris was goddess of the rainbow, along which she travelled to earth as messenger of the gods. (In line 11 below, the same lower-case pun is made on the name of Mercury, another messenger of the gods.)

Line 5, ***loaves and fishes***: Christ's miracle in feeding the multitude (Matthew 14:17–21).

Line 7, ***Galilee's footprints hide a navy of doves***: Christ's footprints in walking on the water (John 6:19) were more productive than a whole navy of the doves sacred to Venus and profane love.

Lines 10–11, ***the avalanche/ Of the golden ghost***: With a suggestion of Danaë, mother of Perseus by Zeus, who visited her in a shower of gold.

Line 11, ***ringed ... her mercury bone***: The sun's courting as a visionary version of putting a ring on her finger, with the reminder that Mercury, messenger of the gods, is also the planet nearest the sun, and the smallest planet.

Line 12, ***hoisted his golden luggage***: The cliché of 'a moonlight flit' in reverse.

Line 14, ***jealous ... unrivalled***: Introducing the ingredient of sexual jealousy but in the only real (*unrivalled*) world, that of human flesh and blood.

50 The hunchback in the park (July 1941) The last poem to be taken from the early Notebooks when Thomas sold them to America. Like the *chained cup* and the *bell*, the hunchback was a memory of Cwmdonkin Park opposite the poet's birthplace in Swansea. In a broadcast ('Reminiscences of Childhood', 1943) he said that he could recall the face of this derelict more clearly 'than the city-street faces I saw an *hour* ago'. The hunchback's name was Oakes. He lived in what would now be called a bed-sit in the Brynmill area of Swansea, but preferred Cwmdonkin to Brynmill park. (Information by courtesy of Gilbert Bennett.) The relationship of the hunchback to the *figure without fault* (line 32) that he creates in his mind parallels the relationship between the imperfect artist and the perfectable work-of-art. In the Notebook version the imagined figure was even said to be a poem. Dylan Thomas is therefore all at once the poet who writes the poem, one of the *truant boys from the town*, and the tormented hunchback himself.

51 Among those Killed in the Dawn Raid was a Man Aged a Hundred (July 1941) Though this war sonnet is characteristic in refusing to let wartime death be vulgarized in pious or propagandist language, it is unusual in its ironic mood: the technology of modern warfare has been used to kill a man already a hundred years old! (Three years later Thomas considered, as a title for the second part of 'Ceremony After a Fire Raid', below, 'Among Those Burned to Death was a Child Aged A Few Hours'.) The irony starts even with the title, a flat headline taken from a newspaper.

Line 3, *locks*: A repeated image in Thomas's wartime poems of the doors of private homes and lives being blown open by the bombs (cf. the *keys* and *locks* of line 8).

Line 3, *where he loved*: 'Where he lived' but also where he probably married and raised a family.

Line 11, *cage*: The rib-cage.

Line 14, *a hundred storks*: Representing new birth, one for each year of his age.

52 Lie still, sleep becalmed (April 1944) A sonnet of sympathy with individual casualties in the Second World War. But its imagery (*sufferer with the wound/ In the throat*) also draws on a much more personal trauma. Ten years previously, in 1933–4, Thomas's father had had treatment for cancer of the mouth, and a draft at the Ohio State University Library and in the Humanities Research Library, Texas, strengthens the connection. It includes the line 'Your wound is a throat' (Thomas always spoke of his father's cancer as of the throat, not of the mouth), the use of 'bandages' where we now have the more poetic *sheets*, and the more recognizably medical opening: 'Lie still, you must sleep.'

Lines 9–11, *Open a pathway ... to the end of my wound*: Spoken by the wounded, asking for help to die.

53 Ceremony After a Fire Raid (May 1944) Stressing the ritualistic pattern (*Begin/ With singing . . . Forgive/Us . . . we chant . . . The masses of the sea*, etc.), Thomas said, 'It really is a Ceremony, and the third part of the poem is the music at the end' (to Vernon Watkins, July 1944). The ceremony also counterpoints images of charring fire and creative water. The milk denied the suckling infant burnt to death with its mother develops in part I into *a great flood* and a *flying sea*, and in part III into the final image of *the infant-bearing sea*. To borrow W. B. Yeats's words in 'The Second Coming', the ceremony of innocence is not drowned but floods again in all the future generations denied birth in the death of this particular child. Part III seems even to owe something direct to Yeats's 'Byzantium'.

Line 4, **Among the street**: The aberrant grammar emphasizes that the singular *street* represents all streets, just as the singular poet is *myselves*, because he represents all the *grievers*.

Line 6, **kneading**: With a pun on 'needing'.

Line 8, **dug**: Both a noun in apposition to *breast* and a verb (*the grave/* [that] *The mother dug*).

Line 14, **a star**: The incendiary bomb, in sad contrast to the star of Bethlehem.

Line 15, **centuries**: The generations that would have come from this child.

Line 33, **I know not**: Section II (the original version of which was titled 'Among Those Burned To Death Was A Child Aged A Few Hours') stresses the irrelevance both of the sex of the child and of the chronology of its death in relation to other deaths, real or mythical, because what the atrocity represents is decreation: *Beginning crumbled back to darkness* (line 58).

Lines 51–2, **the one/ Child**: Christ, who was both the defeat (*nightfall*) of the serpent and the result (*fruit* and *sun* [Son]) of its evil work in Eden.

Line 77, **Glory glory glory**: Both noun (*Glory* [be to] the *ultimate kingdom*) and transitive verb ('Boast the wonder of' the *ultimate kingdom*).

54 Poem in October (August 1944) 'a Laugharne poem: the first place poem I've written' (to Vernon Watkins, August 1944). October was the poet's birth month, and an early morning walk takes him from the Boat House, through the village, and up Sir John's Hill to the west. The view in the last five stanzas is from that hill. Relevant to its visionary, Wordsworthian treatment of childhood is Thomas's remark that he had once long ago even begun a poem entitled 'Ode On The Intimations of Immortality' (to Vernon Watkins, June 1940).

Line 2, **Woke to my hearing**: The subject is *The morning beckon* of line 5.

Lines 19–20, **And the gates/ Of the town closed**: Thirteenth-century Laugharne, a commot of the old Dyfed, would have originally had western and eastern 'gates', but Thomas imagines being let out of the still-portered gates of a medieval city.

Line 32, **the sea wet church**: Laugharne's own ancient church, the other side of the rise of the village, is not visible from Sir John's Hill; therefore, either it is imagined or Thomas is describing the church at Llanybri across the estuary, the burial-place of his aunt Ann Jones of Fernhill. More importantly visible from Sir John's Hill was the area of Fernhill itself, crucial to the childhood memories of 'Poem in October' as of 'Fern Hill' a year later.

Lines 38–40, **There could I marvel . . . but the weather turned around**: The 'marvelling' would have been at the simple contrast between the *summery* weather on the hill and the rain and mist below (stanzas 3 and 4); but the weather *turned around* in a more profound way, cutting back through time itself to the unbroken summers of childhood. A distinction is made between external delight (*marvel*, line 38) and inward vision (*I saw . . . so clearly*, line 46), between fancy (*tall tales*, line 36) and real imagination which, in Coleridge's words, 'dissolves, dissipates in order that it may recreate' (*Biographia Literaria*, ch. 4).

Line 51, **twice told fields**: 'Twice counted', at the time and in the memory. (Given *tall tales* at line 36, there may be a witty reminder of Nathaniel Hawthorne's title *Twice-Told Tales*.)

55 The conversation of prayers (March 1945) Chosen to open Thomas's most famous volume, *Deaths and Entrances* (1946). The imagined drama – that the different prayers (or fears) of a man and a child might be interchanged – draws out the basic meaning of *conversation* as an 'interchange' through speech. Interchange also figures in the poem's criss-crossing of normal end-rhymes with internal-rhymes (*prayers-stairs-tears, said-bed-dead*, etc.). That the man and the child might also be the same person, as in Thomas Hardy's poem 'On One Who Lived and Died Where He Was Born', is carefully allowed for by the syntax: in line 2 the man is 'on the stairs', but the 'child going to bed' would also be there; and in line 8 'the man on the stairs and the child by his bed' raises the question 'Whose bed?'

Line 6, **Turns . . . on**: Completing the cliché started in the first line – that conversations always 'turn on' some subject.

56 A Refusal to Mourn the Death, by Fire, of a Child in London (March 1945) An example of the rhetorical convention of 'occupatio', the poem refuses to do what it then goes on to do – in this case, mourn. The mourning is implicit in the poet's being in deep earnest with his subject, the zeal with which he celebrates the dead girl's survival in the ordinary organic life of the earth. What the poem in reality refuses to do is give voice to a mere local lament (*a grave truth*, line 15), to political propaganda or complacent promises of an afterlife.

Lines 1–10, the main verb is delayed: *Never until . . . Shall I let pray*; and within that main sentence the subject of *tells* is *darkness*, described as 'making mankind', 'fathering bird beast and flower', and 'humbling all'.

Line 12, ***sackcloth***: Biblical, worn for sorrow and mourning (e.g. Genesis 37:34).

Line 15, ***The mankind of her going***: Death is natural (cf. Chaucer's 'no man can undo the law of kind'); but the death of a young girl in wartime brings back a Shakespearean meaning for 'mankind' – that of unnatural cruelty when caused either by or to a female (e.g. *Coriolanus*, IV, ii, 16).

Line 16, ***the stations of the breath***: Evoking the Stations of the Cross, the fourteen stages of Christ's journey to Calvary.

Line 24, ***after the first death***: Either in the ordinary sense that no one dies twice, or with a suggestion of resurrection, or countering the biblical claim that, after the first death, there is the possibility of a 'second death' after judgement (Revelation 21:6–8).

57 This side of the truth (for Llewelyn) (March 1945) Llewelyn was the poet's son, his first child, aged six at this time. Thomas was living in west Wales, but Llewelyn had spent the greater part of the war with his maternal grandmother in Hampshire. The father's advice is therefore in the context of war. Though relevant to a child's inevitable growth from innocence to experience, the phrase *this side of the truth* means more specifically 'this side of death'. Many other Thomas poems stress the presumption of thinking that we can know perfectly how *good and bad* will finally be judged, if at all. 'A Refusal to Mourn the Death, by Fire, of a Child in London', of exactly the same date, is structured on the same message, and the *unminding skies* of line 6 in the present poem makes the same point as the irony in *the discovered skies* of 'How shall my animal', *the answering skies* of 'The conversation of prayers', and *the interpreted evening* of 'Vision and Prayer'. However much man may want to distinguish between Good and Bad, he does so in a completely neutral universe. Nevertheless, the poem's last word is *love*, suggesting that there may be something beyond indifferent nature.

Lines 30–31, *plants/ And animals and birds*: Reminiscent of D. H. Lawrence's 'Birds, Beasts and Flowers', quoted in exactly that order in 'A Refusal to Mourn' above.

Line 32, *Water . . . light . . . earth . . . sky*: The four elements.

58 A Winter's Tale (March 1945) The phrase 'a winter's tale' traditionally describes a non-realistic story told simply to while away a winter's night. But, as in Shakespeare's *The Winter's Tale*, where Mamillius says that 'A sad tale's best for winter', there are tragic as well as fantastic dimensions to the story, with death or near-death being transcended only through love and rebirth. The wintry 'tale' itself is ferried to the poet out of the past on an equally wintry evening and the tale's past-tense narrative is injected at various stages into the present-tense frame of the poem, as follows. Stanzas 1–2, the tale is carried on the incoming twilight into *the river wended vales* where it first took place; stanzas 3–11, the tale starts being told – a man prays for deliverance through love from loneliness and time; stanzas 12–13, addressed to the reader (*Listen . . . Listen*) suggesting that the present-tense landscape is coming to life with the ghosts of people and things from the vanished period of the story itself; stanza 14, the tale proceeds with the appearance of a *she-bird*; stanzas 15–16, addressed to the reader (*Look . . . Look*) again suggesting that the actual period of the tale is coming alive in the present landscape; stanzas 17–22, the tale continues with the man following the she-bird; stanzas 23–4, the past dies back into the landscape; stanzas 25–6, the word 'For' continues the climax of the story from stanza 22, across its interruption by stanzas 23–24.

Lines 42–3, *the bread of water . . . high corn . . . harvest*: A comparison of the snow descending with the manna sent down by God to feed the starving Israelites (Exodus 16).

59 Unluckily for a death In its earlier form (published October 1939) this was titled 'Poem (to Caitlin)'. Thomas completely rewrote it for inclusion in *Deaths and Entrances* (1946). It remained a love poem to his wife but, as Vernon Watkins put it, moved 'away from ironical, and towards religious, statement' (*Letters to Vernon Watkins*, p. 64). The death that has been 'unlucky' is that of an abstract hope in immortality through resurrection (*the phoenix' bid for heaven*) and of an ascetic lover (*the woman in shades*) who waits for him to be her *seducer* only on the other side of the grave. Their bad luck comes from his own good luck in the here-and-now in having Caitlin's physical love. In that love, his *holy lucky body* is already religiously blest (*the ceremony of souls/ Is celebrated there*). The poem is Thomas's version of John Donne's 'The Canonization', where interestingly we also learn that 'The Phoenix riddle hath more wit/ By us, we two being one, are it'.

Line 21, **heroic hosts**: The sexual hospitality of the loved one's body, but with a pun on *hosts* in the sense of the ingredients of the eucharist (the *communion* of line 24).

Line 28, **The death biding two**: The phoenix and the woman in shades.

Line 29, **tigron**: An amalgamation of tiger (*striped*) and lion (*maned*). Mixed identities continue in *androgynous*, *mules*, *minotaurs*, *duck-billed platypus* (though 'duck-billed', a mammal – hence *broody in a milk of birds*), and in the two-headed *phoenix* itself. The monstrous nature of this bestiary symbolizes the perversity that renounces, in favour of future consummation beyond time, *the full assemblage in flower/ Of the living flesh* in the here-and-now.

60 In my craft or sullen art (September 1945) The emphasis on craft, rather than art, is shown by the use of *sullen* as an adjective for the latter, rather than the former (see Introduction). This promotes craft from background into foreground, inverting Shakespeare's image of 'bright metal on a sullen ground' in *I Henry IV*, I, ii, 212. In the same play (at II, iv, 408) Thomas would also have recognized a familiar west Wales dialect word – 'mitching', for playing truant – that he uses in 'Once it was the colour of saying', another pivotal poem about his own poetry. Along with its emphasis on hard-worked craft, the poem is in praise of the only other subject that matters – *the lovers, their arms/ Round the griefs of the ages*. A comment by W. H. Auden is as good an approximation as any to the theme of the poem: 'The impulse to create a work of art is felt when, in certain persons, the passive awe provoked by sacred beings or events is transformed into a desire to express that awe in a rite of worship or homage, and to be fit homage, this rite must be beautiful. This rite has no magical or idolatrous intention; nothing is expected in return' ('Making, Knowing and Judging' in *The Dyer's Hand*).

61 Fern Hill (September 1945) Fernhill is a farm a few miles outside Carmarthen in west Wales, where Thomas spent regular summer holidays as a schoolboy in the 1920s and early 1930s when it was farmed by Ann Jones, the maternal aunt commemorated in 'After the funeral' and in the short story 'The Peaches' in *Portrait of the Artist as a Young Dog*. Now probably his best-loved poem, it had also pleased Thomas: 'it was among the, say, half dozen of mine which came nearest to what I had in heart and mind and muscle when first I wished to write them' (to Marguerite Caetani, November 1949). He thought it 'a poem for evenings and tears' (to David Tennant, August 1945), and its bitter-sweetness was a feature of many works in celebration of childhood written during 1944–45, reflecting a reaction to the obscenities of the war. The poem's form and texture are highly crafted. Along with a regular, patterned syllabic count per line and internal rhymes, the poem uses assonance (vowel-chimes) instead of rhyme at the line-endings (e.g. stanza 1: *boughs–towns, green–leaves, starry–barley, climb–eyes–light*).

Line 9, ***windfall light***: The reflection off early-fallen apples. There is an orchard at the entrance to the farm, but Thomas was also at the time reading D. H. Lawrence's *Collected Poems* and quoted 'O the green glimmer of apples in the orchard/ Lamps in a wash of rain' (to Oscar Williams, July 1945).

Lines 17–18, ***the sabbath rang slowly . . . holy streams***: Evoking the legendary Sabbatic River, which on the seventh day either slowly ceases or slowly starts to flow again. The former, described by Pliny (*Historia Naturalis* XXXI, xviii, 24), was quoted by Thomas in his 1946 broadcast 'The Crumbs of One Man's Year'.

Lines 20–22, ***air . . . watery . . . fire . . . grass***: Involving the four elements. For *fire green as grass* cf. 'bursts up in bonfire green' in D. H. Lawrence's poem 'The Enkindled Spring'.

Line 47, ***by the shadow of my hand***: The syntax scrambles the expression *take me . . . by the . . . hand*, and in the meantime *shadow* also evokes what Wordsworth in 'Mutability' called 'the unimaginable touch of Time'.

Line 51, ***the childless land***: Because the child has grown up and gone away.

Line 54, ***sang in my chains***: Cf. Donne's 'The Triple Fool' – 'Grief brought to numbers cannot be so fierce,/ For, he tames it, that fetters it in verse'.

62 In Country Sleep (April–July 1947) A poem in the tradition of Coleridge's 'Frost at Midnight' and Yeats's 'A Prayer for my Daughter'. On going to sleep, Thomas's four-year-old daughter Aeronwy (born March 1943) is urged not to fear the usual bogey-figures of nightmares or nursery tales (Little Red Riding

Hood, for example – hence, *riding, wolf, hood* and *rosy* in the first stanza). Unlike such tales, the natural world itself does not threaten us. There, what we should heed – not in panic, but in a positive act of recognition – is the fact that maturity and death will always stealthily take away innocence and bounty. In the words of Shakespeare's Sonnet LX, 'And Time that gave doth now his gift confound'. Behind the poem lies the biblical reminder that 'the day of the Lord will come as a thief in the night' (2 Peter 3:10). This was one of the three completed poems (see the next two poems) that Thomas planned as parts of an unfinished work to be called 'In Country Heaven'. Following the earth's self-destruction in an atomic war, people would 'remember places, fears, loves, exultation, misery, animal joy, ignorance, and mysteries, all *we* know and don't know. The poem is made of these tellings. And the poem becomes, at last, an affirmation of the beautiful and terrible worth of the Earth' ('Three Poems', BBC Third Programme, 25 September 1950).

Line 16, ***my rider***: His daughter, *riding far and near* (line 1) in her dreams.

Line 21, ***tolled to sleep***: With a play on 'told to sleep'.

Line 29, ***three Marys***: The three Marys who were present at the crucifixion (Matthew 27:56).

Line 30, ***Sanctum sanctorum***: 'The holy of holies', the innermost part of a Jewish temple.

Lines 43–7, ***Lie in grace . . . Cool in your vows***: Suggesting the ever-widening layers of security under which the child sleeps: under *linen, thatch, lowly house, nimble grove, rosy wood, star* and *wheeling moon*.

Line 96 onwards, ***he comes . . . he comes . . . he comes to take her faith . . . to grieve he will not come***: Echoing a favourite poem by Thomas's favourite modern poet, 'A Broken Appointment' by Thomas Hardy: 'You did not come . . ./ Grieved I, when, as the hope-hour stroked its sum,/ You did not come'.

Lines 97–110: The ending is dominated by words that suggest purpose and control: *designed, truly, ruly, surely*, etc., an emphasis confirmed by two paraphrases in a manuscript now at Texas. The difficult syntax with which the poem ends (an elaborately repeated double negative) stresses that the only thing that the child should fear losing is her knowledge (*faith*) that things will indeed be taken from her.

63 Over Sir John's hill (May–August 1949) Sir John's Hill is a wooded promontory forming the western ascent out of Laugharne. Thomas would have seen it daily to his right as he looked out over the estuary of the rivers Taf and Towy from his Boat House home and the shed where he did his writing. The poem has the same setting and theme as 'Poem on his Birthday', below, but the landscape here is focused specifically – in an allegory of innocence and guilt, judgement and death – on the bird life outside his window. One of the three completed poems (see the previous poem and the next) that Thomas planned as parts of the unfinished work to be called 'In Country Heaven'.

Line 21, **sedge**: Worksheets now at Harvard show Thomas noting that *sedge* (a grass-like plant growing on wet ground) was also a collective noun for herons.

Lines 21–2, **'dilly dilly' . . . killed**: The nursery song 'Mrs Bond' has the lines 'John Ostler, go fetch me a duckling or two;/ Cry Dilly, dilly, dilly, dilly, come and be killed', where *dilly* (a reduplication from 'dally') means 'wait awhile'.

Line 35, **Aesop**: Greek author of fables based on animals.

Line 45, **marks the sparrows hail**: Matthew 10:29.

Line 51, **in the tear of the Towy**: That Thomas meant 'a torn-off' section of the river (*tear* as in 'to tear') is recorded by Gwen Watkins, *Portrait of a Friend*, p. 138. It therefore rhymes with *Wear* in *Wear-willow* at line 58 (from the expression 'wear the willow [garland]', a sixteenth-century expression signifying the loss of a loved one).

Line 58, **grave**: i.e. '[en]grave'.

64 In the White Giant's Thigh (November 1949) Thomas has in mind the White Giant figure, of unknown age, carved into a chalk hill at Cerne Abbas, Dorset, near his mother-in-law's home at Blashford, near Ringwood in Hampshire, where he and his family often stayed. A superstition held that barren girls visiting the figure would conceive. Though the image measures 180 feet from head to foot, it is here imagined as large enough to have a burial-ground in its thigh. The poem imagines the sexual lives of the childless farm women buried there, and the survival of their maternal longings even in death. This is one of the three completed poems (see last two poems) that Thomas planned as parts of the unfinished work to be called 'In Country Heaven'.

Line 1, **many rivers**: The rivers of blood meeting in the curlews' throats.

Line 11, **cudgelling**: The Cerne Abbas Giant wields a huge cudgel.

Line 18, **rough riding boys**: 'Riders of unbroken horses', a phrase celebrated by the 'Rough Riders', the men led by Theodore Roosevelt in the Spanish-American

War of 1898, and in *Rough Riding Romeo*, a successful Tom Mix film of the 1930s. Line 37, **gambo**: The common dialect word in west Wales for a 'hay-cart'.

65 Lament (March 1951) In a version now at Texas, the poem was originally titled 'The Miner's Lament', with images such as 'the skinbare pit' and 'the moon shaft slag'. The phrase *coal black* remains in each stanza, and *black spit*, *wick* and *ram rod*, etc. also remain as traces of the poem's earlier coalmining context, however sexually appropriated the terms themselves may be. This is a useful reminder that in many ways Thomas, though living in rural Laugharne at the end of his career, was a product of the south Wales mining valleys.

66 An old man or a young man (early 1950s) From an untitled fair copy in Thomas's hand now at Texas. Some phrases on the reverse side, in the manner of Thomas's usual worksheets, show that the poem was in progress up to the point of this fair copy. Though the manuscript is undated, the handwriting is of the early 1950s. The poem is clearly in imitation of certain poems by W. B. Yeats.

67 Do not go gentle into that good night (March 1951) Though the survivor of an operation for throat cancer in 1933, from the end of the war to his death in December 1952 Thomas's father suffered chronic ill health. The poet had always respected D. J. Thomas's raging, atheistic independence of mind. This energy now seemed cowed in the face of the double darkness of blindness and death. The main thematic images of rage and of heroic isolation draw on a reading of Yeats and Shakespeare (see individual notes below); but for this painfully personal subject, Thomas also chose the difficult form of the villanelle. Five tercet stanzas are followed by a quatrain stanza; the first and last line of the first stanza then alternate as the last line of the middle four stanzas and are brought together to form a couplet at the end of the final quatrain. And all this on only two rhymes. The challenging stringency of the villanelle is something Thomas would have especially appreciated in the poetry of William Empson. A Thomas parody of Empson's style in 1942 (very much tongue-in-cheek at that stage) had taken the form of a truncated villanelle:

> Not your winged lust but his must now change suit
> The harp-waked Casanova rakes no change
> The worm is (pinpoint) rational in the fruit.

Not girl for bird (gourd being man) breaks root.
Taking no plume for index in love's change
Not your winged lust but his must now change suit.

Desire is phosphorus: the chemic bruit
Lust bears like volts, who'll amplify, and strange
The worm is (pin-point) rational in the fruit.

Line 3, **rage against the dying of the light**: One of several Yeatsian touches (cf. 'raging in the dark' in Yeats's 'The Choice').

Lines 4–13, **wise men . . . Good men . . . Wild men . . . Grave men**: The middle four stanzas, instancing the defiant approach to death of four different types of men, recall section V of Yeats's 'Nineteen Hundred and Nineteen': Thomas is agreeing that the resistance in the face of death of Yeats's 'good', 'wise' and 'great' men is not to be mocked.

Line 5, **had forked no lightning**: 'Had brought no revelation', but cf. also Shakespeare's 'How oft when men are at the point of death/ Have they been merry! which their keepers call/ A lightning before death' (*Romeo and Juliet*, V, iii, 88–90).

Line 14, **gay**: A favourite Yeats word for celebration in the face of tragedy (e.g. in 'Lapis Lazuli').

Line 16, **on the sad height**: Evoking King Lear on the heath and Gloucester on Dover Cliff. Vernon Watkins also recalled Thomas silently acknowledging a reference to Kierkegaard hearing that his father had once stood on a hill cursing God (Gwen Watkins, *Portrait of a Friend*, p. 139).

After his father's death in December 1952, the poet worked on a more specific 'Elegy', unfinished at his own death in America in November 1953. Sheet 2 of 33 numbered sheets now at Texas shows the final stage reached by this very different poem to his father:

Too proud to die, broken and blind he died
The darkest way, and did not turn away,
A cold, kind man brave in his burning pride

On that darkest day. Oh, forever may
He live lightly, at last, on the last, crossed
Hill, and there grow young, under the grass, in love,

Among the long flocks, and never lie lost
Or still all the days of his death, though above
All he longed all dark for his mother's breast

Which was rest and dust, and in the kind ground
The darkest justice of death, blind and unblessed,
Let him find no rest but be fathered and found,

I prayed in the crouching room, by his blind bed,
In the muted house, one minute before
Noon, and night, and light. The rivers of the dead

Moved in his poor hand I held, and I saw
Through his faded eyes to the roots of the sea.
Go calm to your crucifixed hill, I told

The air that drew away from him.

Sheet 30 shows Thomas's plan for the full 'Elegy': '(1) Although he was too proud to die, he did die, blind, in the most agonizing way but he did not flinch from death and was brave in his pride. (2) In his innocence, and thinking he was God-hating, he never knew that what he was was: an old kind man in his burning pride. (3) Now he will not leave my side, though he is dead. (4) His mother said that as a baby he never cried; nor did he, as an old man; he just cried to his secret wound and his blindness, never aloud.'

68 *from* Under Milk Wood The famous 'play for voices' was completed, against time, in the last year of the poet's life, 1953, but it had been a work in progress from at least as early as 1947, and drew on his writings in both poetry and prose from the very beginning – most specifically his broadcast features for the BBC in the 1940s and early 1950s. The play had reached its first reasonably complete form by May 1953 when it was read by a small cast directed and led by Thomas himself (reading the parts of First Voice and the Reverend Eli Jenkins) at the Poetry Center of the Young Men's and Young Women's Hebrew Association in New York City. The play was first broadcast posthumously on the new BBC Third Programme on 25 January 1954. These two excerpts show how poems take their place in the wide range of literary forms (monologue, dialogue, song, children's games, nursery rhymes) employed within the poetic-prose narrative of the whole. Eli Jenkins's hymn to the morning towards the beginning of the play parodies poems in praise of place or event common in county-newspaper verse, but with a technical skill that runs away with the parody. Towards the end of the play, the stanzas exchanged between the dead Rosie Probert and the blind Captain Cat are at the heart of Dylan Thomas's own favourite part of the work.

69 Poem on his Birthday (Autumn 1949–Summer 1951) The 'house on stilts' of line 4 is both the cliff-perched Boat House in Laugharne where Thomas and his family lived from 1949 and the precariously perched shed nearby where he did his writing. Thomas is responding to the luminous views over the estuaries of the rivers Taf and Towy and contemplating the waterside and marine life before him. The beautiful prospect also includes strong emblems of death, not only in the natural world but in the unnatural threat of a Third, atomic World War (the *hammer flame* and *rocketing wind* of stanzas 5 and 8), and not only in his own death but that of fellow human beings whom he sees in the last stanza as *angels* and *shining men*.

Line 8, ***thirty-fifth wind turned age***: 'half his bible span' as he put it in a synopsis given to Bill Read (*The Days of Dylan Thomas*, 1964). The poem was probably begun in October 1949, but a worksheet at Harvard is titled 'Poem in October (1950)' and the poem was not in fact finished until 1951.
Line 23, ***wynds***: Dialect word for 'alleys'.
Line 38, ***angelus***: In the Roman Catholic church an angelus bell signals the times for a series of prayers commemorating the Annunciation and Incarnation.
Line 85, ***nimbus***: A bright cloud or halo.

Index of Titles and First Lines

(Titles of poems are in italics. Where the first line is exactly the same as the title, the first line is not repeated.)